M000310447

THE NEW
SOCIOLOGY
OF KNOWLEDGE

THE NEW
SOCIOLOGY
OF KNOWLEDGE

*The Life
and Work of
Peter L. Berger*

Michaela Pfadenhauer

With selected essays by Peter L. Berger

Translated from the German
by Miriam Geoghegan

Transaction Publishers
New Brunswick (U.S.A.) and London (U.K.)

Library of Congress Catalog Number: 2012036152
ISBN: 978-1-4128-4989-0
Printed in the United States of America

Library of Congress Cataloging-in-Publication Data

Pfadenhauer, Michaela, 1968-
  [Peter L. Berger. English]
  The new sociology of knowledge : the life and work of Peter L. Berger / Michaela Pfadenhauer; with selected essays by Peter L. Berger.
     p. cm.
  Includes bibliographical references and index.
  ISBN 978-1-4128-4989-0
  1. Berger, Peter L., 1929- 2. Sociologists--Biography. 3. Knowledge, Sociology of. 4. Religion and sociology. I. Berger, Peter L., 1929- II. Title.
  HM479.B47.P43 2013
  301.092--dc23
  [B]
                                                           2012036152

Contents

Preface

Can one call an author a classic during his lifetime? Or even a classic of the sociology of knowledge? These questions were not asked by me. Rather, they were posed by Peter L. Berger in the summer of 2006 in reply to my e-mail requesting his permission to write a book about him for the German series "Classics of the Sociology of Knowledge." As Berger still comes to Europe several times a year, I got to know him personally soon after this initial electronic contact. In the summer of 2008 I visited him at the Institute on Culture, Religion and World Affairs (CURA) at Boston University. And in the summer of the following year I had an opportunity to attend a CURA summer course. Eventually I succeeded in dispelling his doubts. I argued that a large number of his works were characterized by a sociology-of-knowledge perspective—and that, what is more, he and his coauthor, Thomas Luckmann, would be more than entitled to refer to their book *The Social Construction of Reality* (1966a) as a classic without running the risk of being accused of vanity.

Because sociology lacks an undisputed methodological and thematic identity, classical sociological thinkers play a key role in fostering and underpinning a sense of identity among sociologists. In this sense, the volumes in a series on classical sociologists, in which the German-language version of this book appeared, constitute what Dirk Kaesler (1999: 31) calls a "tribal history" of the discipline. Now, Peter L. Berger views any form of group affiliation with suspicion. And, to put it mildly, he considers sociologists to be quite a boring tribe. Kaesler notes (ibid., 30) that classical sociological thinkers are not "born" but "made," and that their "classicity" is grounded in a need felt by contemporary sociologists. I, too, share this need. At the same time, however, I am aware that I am imposing quite a burden on Berger by "making" him a classic in his own lifetime.

The inestimable advantage of writing a book about a *living* classic is that one can ask him about various aspects that are difficult—if not impossible—to reconstruct from his publications. What is more, one gains fruitful biographical insights and valuable background information about his works in the process. The downside is that a living classic can defend himself vigorously if he is unhappy with the way he and his works are represented. Peter L. Berger made little use of his right of complaint. This is probably due less to the absence of cause for complaint than to the fact that humor-lover Berger, who has written a whole book on humor (Berger 1997a), is convinced that "all autobiographical (or, to coin an adjective, 'autobibliographical') reflection presupposes a deficient sense of humor" (1986d: 221). Indeed, his willingness to allow himself to be pestered with questions was practically boundless. The only time I felt I was really getting on his nerves was when I asked him about his thoughts on hell. (It was not even my idea; my fellow students in the CURA summer course put me up to it.) I would like, therefore, to take this opportunity to express my heartfelt gratitude to him for his willingness to meet me halfway—literally and metaphorically.

Alfred Schutz (1976: 274) distinguishes between two variants of responsibility: "being responsible *for*" something one has done, and "being responsible *to*" someone. Even though the responsibility for the content of this book rests solely with me, I could not have managed without the help of others. Hans-Georg Soeffner and Winfried Gebhardt deserve explicit mention. Bernt Schnettler and Hubert Knoblauch provided valuable encouragement. However, most of what I believe to have understood from and about Peter L. Berger was unlocked in conversation with Ronald Hitzler, to whom I owe an additional debt of thanks, because it was he who gave me the idea to write this book in the first place.

It is thanks to Peter L. Berger's mediation that this book can now be made available to an English-speaking audience. When Berger contacted Transaction Publishers on my behalf, Chairman and Editorial Director Irving Louis Horowitz immediately expressed interest in publishing the work. I am indebted to his wife, Transaction President Mary Curtis Horowitz, for her wholehearted support for the project after her husband's passing. At Irving Louis Horowitz's suggestion, the book has been expanded to include five of Berger's own texts. Selected by the author himself, they address in condensed form key aspects dealt with in the thematic chapters (1–5).

Chapter 1—"Beginnings of the New Sociology of Knowledge: Influences, Teachers, and Collaborators"—has been supplemented with Peter L. Berger's "Reflections on the Twenty-Fifth Anniversary of *The Social Construction of Reality*" (1992), in which he recalls the genesis of this classic work in productive collaboration with Thomas Luckmann. He notes with satisfaction that the paradigm developed in *Social Construction*—which links institutional structures and processes with processes of consciousness—had shown itself to be eminently useful in his later research, which focused not on social theory but on phenomena such as modernity, desecularization, and economic culture.

"Pluralism, Protestantization, and the Voluntary Principle" (2007), a chapter that Berger contributed to a book entitled *Democracy and the New Religious Pluralism*, rounds off the second chapter of the present book, which is devoted to "Modernity and Pluralism." In his contribution, Berger makes it clear that, while modernity is not intrinsically secularizing, it does go hand in hand with pluralism. Under conditions of pluralism, not only religious convictions but all cognitive and normative definitions of reality lose their hitherto inherent status of certainty and unquestionability. Hence, a grave consequence of modernization is that well-nigh all aspects of human existence cease to be a matter of fate and become a matter of choice.

Chapter 3—"Religion and Desecularization"—is complemented by "The Desecularization of the World" (1999), an essay Berger contributed to *The Desecularization of the World. Resurgent Religion and World Politics*, which he edited. In this essay, Berger discusses the connection between modernity and the worldwide resurgence of religion—especially of conservative, orthodox, and traditionalist religious movements. Underlining the striking differences between these movements, and their correspondingly different stances vis-à-vis modernity, Berger addresses the fundamentally important role they play on the global political stage—in ideological and military conflicts, economic development, human rights, and social justice.

Chapter 4—"Culture and Socioeconomic Change"—is enhanced by a short essay entitled "Our Economic Culture" (1994) in which Berger explains the concept of economic culture as understood by the Institute for the Study of Economic Culture (ISEC)—presently called CURA—which he founded at Boston University in 1985. He uses three research projects conducted under the auspices of ISEC to illustrate the basic stance, line of inquiry, and some of the categories that he and his collaborators adopted when investigating the cultural framework of economic activities.

With the inclusion in Chapter 5—"Knowledge and Reality"—of a journal article by Peter L. Berger entitled "Identity as a Problem in the Sociology of Knowledge" (1966), the present book comes full circle, returning to the subject of social theory. In the article, Berger shows the theoretical gains to be achieved by integrating the sociology of knowledge with Meadian social psychology. Social psychology in the Meadian tradition is concerned with the dialectic between social structure and psychological reality: The individual realizes himself in society; he recognizes his identity in social categories; and these categories become reality as he lives in society. The sociology of knowledge, by contrast, concerns itself with the dialectic between social structure and the "worlds" in which people live: People in societies produce "worlds" whose conceptual modalities become unquestionably certain knowledge. In this way, these worlds become objective reality for their inhabitants. And, as Berger concludes, *"identity . . . is always identity within a specific, socially constructed world."*

What was a joint endeavor from the start has become even more so by the inclusion of these original Berger texts.

A final word of thanks goes to Miriam Geoghegan, my translator and fellow sociologist, who shares Berger's conviction that sociology can—and should—be presented in intelligible language. She made sure that most of the sociologese to which I am prone got lost in translation.

Introduction and Biographical Overview

In his essay on Emile Durkheim as a "classical sociological thinker," René König (1976: 312–13) lists three possible approaches to writing such a piece. First, one can present the classical sociologist's oeuvre against the historical background of its time and identify its motivation and impact; second, one can focus on his contribution to a *"sociologia perennis"*; and finally, one can identify and assess his "immanent or explicit philosophy." König rules out *a priori* a fourth variant—a mere précis—because, in his view, it would not do justice to a classical thinker who, by definition, "developed not only his own worldview but also his own stylistic device" (our translation).

Dirk Kaesler (1999: 30) defines a classical sociologist as someone whose "works occupied a central position among the sociological ideas and notions of an era and were therefore the focus of sociological discourse." Following this criterion, the objective of the present book is to demonstrate the relevance of Berger's oeuvre to the sociology of knowledge. It goes without saying that *The Social Construction of Reality* (Berger & Luckmann 1966a)—which laid the foundations for the new sociology of knowledge—will occupy a prominent position (Chapter 5). A further objective of this critical appraisal is to draw the attention of the sociologically interested reader to Berger's other works. My aim in so doing is to help reverse the tendency to view the later Berger solely as a sociologist of religion—or even merely as a theologically informed religious author—rather than as a thematically versatile sociologist whose works are characterized by an explicit, or at least an implicit, sociology-of-knowledge perspective.

Peter L. Berger stands out among his fellow social scientists both quantitatively and qualitatively. Quantitatively, because he definitely belongs to the prolific-writer category. He has written numerous monographs, which have been translated into many languages, and a multitude of essays in scholarly journals and popular magazines; he has edited countless collected volumes. However, Berger is also an exceptional scientist from a *qualitative* point of view. For decades, he has played a role in shaping—or, indeed, determining—both public debate and social scientific discourse in America and far beyond.

As a sociologist, Berger has played three roles: as a theoretician of modern life, an analyst of modern religiosity, and an empiricist of global economic culture. His sociological works can be grouped into three categories: modernity and pluralism (Chapter 2 below), religion and (Chapter 3), and culture and socioeconomic change (Chapter 4). In all three areas, the focus on processes (rather than on the status quo) is characteristic of Berger's thinking.

For all the thematic fields that Berger has tilled over the years, it should not be forgotten that he has also written introductory books and general overview articles on sociology. Foremost among these publications are his *Invitation to Sociology* (1963a), which, in the opinion of many colleagues, is still "unrivaled" (Schnettler 2006: 54); *Sociology—A Biographical Approach* (1972), a textbook coauthored with his wife Brigitte; and *Sociology Reinterpreted* (1981), which was coauthored with his brother-in-law, Hansfried Kellner. Even this short list suffices to show that Berger is not a lone writer. His collaboration with Thomas Luckmann, for example, has yielded two monographs and three essays. In later years he coauthored works with Richard Neuhaus, Samuel Huntington, Gracie Davie, and Anton Zijderveld, to name but a few.

For Manfred Prisching (2001: 12), Berger's book *Redeeming Laughter. The Comic Dimension in Human Experience* (1997a) is "an exception." Although Berger himself notes in the preface (ibid., ix) that the "underlying argument and the finale are religious," the book does not quite fit in with the other themes that Berger has dealt with during the course of his life. While it is definitely not the key to his oeuvre, it could well be a key to understanding him as a person, as the following quotation suggests:

> I have been obsessed with the question of the nature of the comic all my life, ever since my father,[1] an inveterate teller of jokes, encouraged me to tell my own about the time when I entered kindergarten, where, according to reliable sources, I made a nuisance of myself as I faithfully followed the paternal mandate. Sooner or later, I had to write this book. (1997a: x)[2]

Last, but not least, it should not be forgotten that Berger has written two novels—*The Enclaves* (1965a) and *Protocol of a Damnation* (1975)—which, in his view, deserved more attention than they received (however, cf. Mechling 1986). He wrote the first novel under a pseudonym for fear of damaging his reputation as a serious scholar. The second book was, as he says himself, the product of boredom during a semester spent at the University of Cologne at the invitation of René König, whom I mentioned at the beginning of this chapter. Berger's unwillingness to while away his time unproductively was also what motivated him to put his memories of his childhood and youth down on paper while immobilized with a foot injury. Although, at the time, he had no intention of publishing them, he eventually did (2008a). While, for Berger, writing is not merely a way of passing the time, it seems to cost him a lot less effort than most.[3] His restlessness during the period between books subsides only when the draft of the next one has taken shape. Even before the appearance of *In Praise of Doubt* (2009)—a book coauthored with Anton Zijderveld—Berger had hatched the idea for a second autobiographical work, *Adventures of an Accidental Sociologist* (2011), in which he constructs the genesis of his own oeuvre.

Although quite accustomed to success, Berger noted first with surprise, and then with increasing skepticism, the Austrian media coverage of the publication of the aforementioned autobiographical memoirs of his childhood and youth, *Im Morgenlicht der Erinnerung* ("In the Morning Light of Memory") (2008a). The book's appearance coincided with the award of the Paul Watzlawick Ring of Honor by the Vienna Medical Chamber, who acclaimed him as a "personality of international standing." It was probably no coincidence that the award also coincided with the seventieth anniversary of the *Anschluss*—that is, the annexation of Austria by Germany in 1938. This prompted Berger, in all the interviews he gave, to emphatically refuse to be stylized as a victim of Nazism. It was precisely because of his Jewish roots that Berger, whose parents had become Protestants in 1938, initially hesitated to publish his memoir. He feared that Jewish friends might feel snubbed by what they felt was a decision against a Jewish identity on his part.

A characteristic trait of Peter L. Berger's is revealed here. Like Ulrich, the central protagonist of Robert Musil's novel *The Man Without Qualities* (1995 [1930ff.]), he finds all forms of group subsumption suspect—irrespective of whether the group in question is a majority or a minority.[4] It is of the utmost importance to him that he not be pigeonholed in a collective category—be it victim of Nazism, Jewish émigré, confessed Christian, or conservative intellectual. In his view, collectivism is a cheap solution to the problem of developing systems of classification for the modern world and the modern personality. As in Musil's case, the "merging of the perpetually quarreling selves in a dreamed unity" of collective identity provides little consolation to Berger (cf. 1992b: 117).

In his first memoir (2008a), Berger recalls a mainly happy childhood and youth. Because of the many options revealed in his biography—or, to put it existentially, because modern man is condemned to freedom—Berger regards it as a case study of the situation of modern man.

This memoir finally put paid to the frequent claim that Peter L. Berger was born in Trieste, Italy, in 1929. As a child he did spend every summer in Italy, the home country of his mother's side of the family, and he does speak Italian, but he is a native of Vienna. And despite his forced emigration via Palestine to the United States, he still feels a close attachment to the city of his birth. What is more, not only does he have good memories of his childhood in Vienna, the city also shaped his identity to such an extent that, when I asked him about the difference between himself and Thomas Luckmann, he described himself and his colleague as the two opposite poles of *Austrian* culture. One (Berger), with his liking for a luxurious, urbane ambiance, is a typical manifestation of the Viennese coffeehouse intellectual, while the other (Luckmann), with his love of nature and his passion for fishing, is a typical example of an Austrian-Slovenian mountain hermit.

In hindsight, Berger sees the years in Palestine as a search for a religious identity that came to an end when he arrived in the promised land, America, in 1946 (2008a: 201). With the same conviction with which he gave his national identity as Austrian when entering Palestine in 1938, he stated his religious affiliation as Lutheran Protestant when entering the United States. Strongly influenced by a "religiosity of Lutheran coloration" (2008a: 134; our translation) during his two years at a Swiss mission school in Haifa, and impressed by the "rousing way" in which the Neumanns, a couple with whom Berger's family had become friends, practiced their Christianity, he was introduced to a distinctly un-European approach to religious practice.[5] Rather than committing himself to just one church community, he chose a church—first Presbyterian, then Anglican—on the basis of the service on offer. Berger's self-study of theological and philosophical literature was at least equally important for the development of his religious identity. His main mentor was Fritz Neumann, with whom he had a lot in common, especially a fascination with Kierkegaard. Berger acquired a knowledge of Lutheran theology through reading the books from a library left behind by Pastor Berg of the German Lutheran Church. This fostered a development that he describes as a "paradox":

> Without having had contact with a single Lutheran, I made up a Lutheranism of my own. However, it was a replica molded by reason, and I later realized that it was not true to the original. But, even now, I would still say that, emotionally, I was not far off the mark. Thus, when I acquired a deeper knowledge of Lutheranism over the years, I was able to verify my original findings. Although my theological understanding has become much more liberal in the meantime, and I cannot, therefore, subscribe to the full text of the Augsburg Confession, I would say that, despite many reservations, I am much more a Lutheran than any other type of Christian. Perhaps—and may Spinoza forgive me for this—I discovered my *anima naturaliter lutherana*. (2008a: 189–90; our translation)

On his arrival in New York, Berger was intent on studying theology in order to realize what he felt to be his vocation: to become a Lutheran minister. He earned a bachelor of arts degree from Wagner College on Staten Island, an institution that he describes as "only nominally Lutheran" (2008a: 213). Berger supplemented his studies there with a sojourn at a college in Ohio. Although he was then entitled to study at a theological faculty, he felt that, as an immigrant, he should first learn more about American society. Sociology seemed to him to be a good way of doing that. As the New School was the only university in New York at which he could study in the evening, thereby allowing him to work full-time to earn his living, he enrolled in a master's program there. The first course he attended was entitled "Balzac as a Sociologist" and was taught by Albert Salomon. Berger stresses that there was basically nothing to be said against using Balzac to introduce students to sociology, because the author had intended his novels to provide a picture of French society. However, as he recalls with a chuckle, the consequence was that after a semester during which he wrote, among other things, a term paper comparing Balzac's *Illustrious Gaudissart* with Arthur Miller's new play *Death of a Salesman,* he had found out hardly anything about contemporary American society.

Berger's decision to enroll at the New School was to prove a serendipitous one, nonetheless. In the 1950s, the Graduate Faculty of the New School was a haven for European intellectuals who had fled from fascism. Founded in 1933 as the European University in Exile, it was renamed the Graduate Faculty of Political and Social Science in 1934, and is now known as the New School for Social Research. There, Berger came into direct contact with the tradition of the European humanities and social sciences, whereas his encounter with contemporary American sociology was merely second-hand. Had he not been introduced to classical sociological theory, it is unlikely that he would have become hooked on the discipline, because contemporary American sociology had failed to capture his interest.

Apart from Albert Salomon, the two teachers at the Graduate Faculty of the New School who exerted a major influence on Berger were Carl Mayer and Alfred Schutz (see Chapter 1 below). After earning his master's degree in sociology from the New School in 1950, and spending a year at the Lutheran Theological Seminar in Philadelphia, he abandoned his plans to become a Lutheran minister, deciding instead to return to the New School to do a doctorate. He received his PhD in 1952 for a dissertation entitled "The Baha'i Movement: A Contribution to the Sociology of Religion."

Because he was drafted into the US army in 1953, Berger had to forgo working on a research project on religion and the churches in post-war Germany directed by Carl Mayer. On Berger's recommendation, Thomas Luckmann took his place on the team. Berger first met Luckmann at a philosophy seminar at the New School given by Karl Löwith; the two men have been close friends and scholarly collaborators ever since (see Chapter 1 below). Although Berger had to withdraw from Mayer's project, he was to receive an invitation after his discharge from the army two years later to undertake a research project at the Protestant Academy in the German town of Bad Boll, near Stuttgart in southwest Germany. This would bring him not only to Germany but also to the subject of religion and church in Germany.

Although Berger detested the basic-training phase of his military service—during his school days he and some friends had formed an "anti-sport league"[6]—he was lucky insofar as he was drafted during the period between the Korean and Vietnam Wars. Moreover, because he was deployed as a "social worker" in a psychiatric clinic,[7] he not only had a nine-to-five job, but also one that enabled him to rub shoulders with a cross-section of American society.

After returning from Germany in mid-1956, Berger had to spend some months in a non-academic job. However, he was drawn to the academic world—or, more precisely, to the American academic world. To this day, he considers the American higher education landscape to be much more conducive to what he calls "intellectual entrepreneurship" than its German or Austrian counterparts. Intellectual entrepreneurship is the term Berger uses to refer to a project that, in fact, originated in the prolific nature and the success of his writing, although it really took off with the foundation of CURA's predecessor, the Institute for the Study of Economic Culture (ISEC) at Boston University in 1985.

The first milestone in Berger's academic career—his appointment as an associate professor at the Graduate Faculty of the New School in 1963—was preceded by posts at the University of North Carolina and the Hartford Seminary Foundation. Although Berger indicated to me that he did not consider the years at the Women's College of the University of North Carolina (1956–58) and at the Hartford Theological Seminary (1958–63) to be worthy of further mention, they were probably of some importance for his development as a university teacher. This can be seen from his striking description of the experience—or "culture shock"—of the "sense of precarity" that all social scientists should possess, but that, with increasing professionalization, becomes routine:

> To a degree this is probably inevitable. After all, one cannot live all the time with one's mouth open. This is why teaching, and especially the occasional teaching of introductory courses, is a salutary activity for the professional social scientist. In the reactions of the students to what he presents he can re-experience the freshness of the "sociological imagination,"[8] sometimes even its liberating quality. The experience of beginning students (needless to say, it is the brighter students who are at issue here!) affords a good illustration of the nature of the shock which the social sciences are capable of administering. (1961: 15)

Despite the many student crushes that he probably encountered as a young lecturer in a women's college, North Carolina was not an environment that Berger could imagine living in for long—not least because of the manifest racial discrimination that still prevailed there in the 1950s, and that had already left a bad taste in his mouth during his military service. In Hartford, Connecticut, by contrast, he encountered what was for him quite a pleasant, ecumenically oriented

Protestant milieu. However, the longing to teach and work at a sociological rather than a theological faculty became increasingly urgent. In retrospect, Berger describes his most successful book, *Invitation to Sociology* (1963a), as being strongly motivated by a desire to attract the attention of his fellow sociologists. If this really was the case,[9] the strategy certainly worked.

The appointment to the post of assistant professor at his alma mater meant that two wishes came true for Berger. First, he got to teach sociology students, and second, during the first few years at least, he encountered the stimulating intellectual climate for which the Graduate Faculty of the New School had become famous during and after the Second World War. When he was appointed chairman of the Sociology Department some years later, he endeavored to restore this climate by hiring European sociologists. The idea was to bring a bit of heterogeneity into the professorships, which, after the passing of the founding generation, were now held almost entirely by American scholars. The failure of these efforts was to put an end to this stage in Berger's career. He left the New School in 1970.

Stimulated by lively discussions during the courses he taught at the New School—as in his student days, they were still held mainly in the evening—Berger intensified his sociological publishing activities, for the most part in coauthorship with Thomas Luckmann, Hansfried Kellner, Stanley Pullberg, or Maurice Natanson. Together with Berger, these men formed what he jestingly refers to as the "clique" (2011: 80) that developed the concept for *The Social Construction of Reality* (Berger & Luckmann 1966a). However, even during those years, Berger's interest in issues relating to the sociology of religion and to theology persisted. Besides numerous articles and essays in journals and popular media, he published two very successful books—*The Sacred Canopy* (1967) and *A Rumor of Angels* (1969a).

This period also saw the beginning of Berger's political activities. In the late 1960s he protested against America's Indochina policy. However, his protest was not motivated by the left-wing *zeitgeist* but rather by his criticism of the way America was waging the war in Vietnam. Hence, he joined the national steering committee of an organization called Clergy and Laymen Concerned about Vietnam (CALCAV), which strictly opposed the Vietnam War.

Fearing that Latin America could become a further site for comparable American interventions, Berger's interest in the development problems of the so-called Third World grew. He left the New School in 1970 to take up a professorship at Rutgers University in New Jersey, which he would hold until 1979. By 1970 at the latest, modernization and the confrontation with Marxism, socialism, and capitalism as a framework for political and economic development had become key themes for him and have remained so ever since. He describes as a pivotal experience his encounter in 1969 with Ivan Illich, who invited him to give a seminar at the Centro Intercultural de Documentación ("Intercultural Documentation Center") in Cuernavaca, Mexico. In the course of his discursive engagement with Illich's strong criticism of modernization, Berger came to explicitly endorse market economy principles and democracy as the primary engines of progress.

This stance—to wit, Berger's refusal to be hijacked by those who misinterpreted *The Social Construction of Reality* (Berger & Luckmann 1966a) as a theoretical guide to revolution for the leftist protest movement—and the initiation of the so-called Hartford Appeal for Theological Affirmation reinforced his conservative image in the 1970s. In the Hartford Appeal (also known as the Hartford Declaration), which was drawn up and distributed in 1975 and published in 1976 (Berger & Neuhaus 1976c), the twenty-three signatories—mainly prominent Christian intellectuals—repudiated a number of secularist attitudes in contemporary Christian theology. The appeal was intended as a protest against the *zeitgeist* and as a stance *Against the World for the World*.[10] Here, Berger played not only the role of a religious individual but also that of a political actor, deploying his theory of the sociology of knowledge for his own ends, as it were. The criticism, voiced in unison with like-minded people, was aimed at halting what they deemed to be an unfortunate development and at initiating a spiritual shift. It opposed a Protestantism that, in their view, had become inextricably entangled in modernity and, as the historian of religion Rudolf Otto would have put it, had lost the "transcendence of the holy" in the process. Berger and his coauthors were children of their time. In other words, they were shaped by a particular sociocultural context that fostered the *zeitgeist* against which the Hartford Appeal was directed. However, as Berger himself points out, the fact that human thinking is socially determined should not be misconstrued as mechanistic, inevitable, or inexorable social determinism. Rather, the relationship between ideas and society must be apprehended as a dialectical one: "Ideas come out of a context, but they also act back upon that context" (Berger & Neuhaus 1976d: 17).[11]

More often than the role of activist, Berger played the part of an intellectual adviser who was not afraid of associating with politics, the church, or industry. In the 1980s, he felt provoked by the anti-smoking movement (1986c), and especially by what he considered to be its ideological output on the health hazards of passive smoking (1988d). Between 1979 and 1987, he acted as a consultant to the tobacco industry, visiting several World Health Organization (WHO) conferences as an undercover participant observer. The WHO was the organization under whose umbrella the initiative that Berger (1988d: 83) refers to as the "international antismoking conglomerate" developed. He reconstructed the convictions of the anti-smoking movement as "ideology"—in other words, as ideas that are not based on scientific argument but are rooted in culture and entangled with vested interests. Observing the anti-smoking phenomenon in the broad social context of developments such as the health cult, the obsession with youth, the environmental and consumer-protection movements, and risk paranoia, he provides a cameo empirical lesson in the micro- and macrosociology of knowledge.

The second milestone in Berger's academic career came in 1981, when he took up an appointment as professor at Boston University. Howard Kee, a colleague at Boston College, where Berger had taught for two years after relocating to Boston in 1979,[12] and John Silber, the then president of Boston University, were major driving forces behind this appointment. Moreover, these two men were instrumental in helping Berger to realize his vision of intellectual entrepreneurship by founding the Institute for the Study of Economic Culture (ISEC) in 1985. Silber authorized Berger to start the research center in order to convince him to stay on at the university; he had heard from Howard Kee that Berger was negotiating with Southern Methodist University in Texas.

Berger's book *The Capitalist Revolution: Fifty Propositions about Prosperity, Equality, and Liberty* (1986a) appeared in 1986. In a sense, it can be read as the agenda of the new institute. Its neo-Weberian research question about the relationship between culture and economic development involved political consequences insofar as Berger considered democratization tendencies to be a likely consequence of increased prosperity, and argued that economic progress precedes political progress. Or, as he succinctly puts it, "Capitalism is a necessary but not sufficient condition of democracy" (ibid., 81).

The institute's initial research projects focused mainly on the implications and consequences of dominant religious movements in specific regions of the world, for example Pentecostalism in Latin America and

Africa, and (Neo)-Confucianism in Asia. In 2001, the Pew Charitable Trusts designated the University of Boston as one of "ten centers of excellence for the interdisciplinary study of religion," and awarded it a $2.5-million grant to set up the Institute on Religion and World Affairs (IRWA). Berger's institute ISEC underwent its first name change and extended the scope of its research to the interaction between culture and development. The second name change occurred in 2003, when IRWA was renamed CURA, the Institute on Culture, Religion and World Affairs. The thematic orientation—the question of the "elective affinity" between sociocultural change and economic development in various regions of the world—remained the same. Thanks to his ability to generate sponsor interest in this research question—Pew Charitable Trusts is a particularly affluent example—Berger has procured a large number of projects for the institute during its twenty-five-year history. On July 1, 2009, at the age of eighty, he handed over the directorship of CURA to his colleague Robert Hefner, whom he now assists in an advisory capacity.

Berger's enormous, and rarely diminishing, productivity over the last fifty years is by no means due only to this indisputable talent as a writer—although, thanks to this talent, intellectual activity probably comes easier to him than to most people. Rather, his productivity can be explained by the dual motivation to describe phenomena in a value-free way and to gain a deep understanding of their ethical implications. Hence, the present book could bear the subtitle "The Sociologist as a Moralist" that René König (1976) used in his essay on Emile Durkheim as a classical sociological thinker, which I mentioned at the beginning of this chapter. Indeed, Berger makes no bones about his moral stance. In *Pyramids of Sacrifice. Political Ethics and Social Change* (1974a: 246) he confesses:

> . . . that I have rarely been able to sustain an attitude of permanent disengagement, even though I find it important that such an attitude be assumed temporarily for purposes of scientific understanding. In other words, I deem it both feasible and desirable to view the social and political realities of our time *sine ira et studio*; but, for myself, at any rate, it seems to be neither feasible nor desirable to persist in this posture of detachment. Over and over again I find myself propelled out of detachment by the moral urgencies of the historical situation. I suppose this means that, at heart, I am a moralist.

However, his sociology-of-knowledge attitude, which is as characteristic of Berger as his moral stance, acts as a counterbalance to the latter (see Chapter 6 below).

Notes

1. It is only logical, therefore, that the book should be dedicated to the memory of his father.

2. Although not the subject of his research, Berger recalls the black humor of undertakers, which he encountered when he dealt briefly with occupational sociology issues at an early stage in his career (cf. Berger & Lieban 1960, Berger 1954a, and Pfadenhauer 2003).

3. Hence, while writing the present book, I received cautious but persistent enquiries from Berger about the "the current state of play."

4. I would like to thank Hans-Georg Soeffner for drawing my attention to this key to understanding Berger.

5. The term un-European is employed here not in a pejorative sense, but rather in allusion to the differences between religious America and the "Eurosecularity" that Peter L. Berger, Grace Davie, and Effie Fokas (2008b) have identified. While belonging without believing tends to be more common in Europe, un-European refers to the habit of choosing and switching between service offerings within easy reach, which is not really a typical practice in Europe. In Germany at least, church membership generally implies being a member of a local church community and attending that church's services—if one attends church at all.

6. Berger's aversion to physical exercise dates back to his early youth—the first friends he made in Palestine were three classmates "who conspired with him against sports" (2008a: 152; our translation).

7. The sergeant who took down his particulars when he was inducted did not quite know what a "sociologist" was. So he registered Berger as a "social worker."

8. Berger borrowed the term "sociological imagination" from C. Wright Mills (1959), whose paradigmatic work of the same name he frequently quotes (e.g., 1994).

9. Berger's explanation may be an ex-post construction because, overall, he appears to have been less strategically minded career-wise than he pretends to be here.

10. This was title of the book edited by Peter L. Berger and Richard Neuhaus (1976a) in which the Hartford Appeal was published. The book was subtitled: *The Hartford Appeal and the Future of American Religion.*

11. However, it is difficult for the individual actor to make out his location in this dialectic flow. According to Berger (loc. cit.), this observation can be viewed as a sociology-of-knowledge comment on the Christian mission formulated in Ecclesiastes 11: 1: "Cast thy bread upon the waters; for thou shalt find it after many days."

12. Berger's decision to relocate to Boston was prompted by the fact that his wife Brigitte had been offered a post as sociology chairman at Wellesley College (2011: 155). It took quite a while before he felt at home there. New York was for him the epitome of a city, and indeed of urbanity per se; it was a place where anything could happen—at any time. When reading "New York City 1976: A Signal of Transcendence" (1977b), one gets an idea of just how hard he must have found it to leave New York.

1

Beginnings of the New Sociology of Knowledge: Influences, Teachers, and Collaborators

The clarity and frequency with which Peter L. Berger refers in his works to the intellectual currents that nurtured his sociology testifies to the influence of the sociology of knowledge on his self-concept. These references reveal—to others and to himself—that he is a child of a particular time, and that he acknowledges the *zeitgeist* that shaped his thinking. The intellectual traditions that influenced Berger most are associated mainly with the names Max Weber, Emile Durkheim, Karl Marx, Arnold Gehlen, George Herbert Mead, Alfred Schutz, and William James.[1]

The "theory for the sociology of knowledge" formulated in *The Social Construction of Reality. A Treatise in the Sociology of Knowledge* (Berger & Luckmann 1966a: 185) is a systematic integration of key elements of interpretive sociology, structural functionalism, early Marx's philosophy of history, symbolic interactionism, philosophical anthropology, and phenomenology. While Berger's main influence was Max Weber, his coauthor Thomas Luckmann's thinking was shaped more by Alfred Schutz's mundane phenomenology, even before he systematized the Schutzian approach in *The Structures of the Life-World* (Schutz & Luckmann 1973).

The following statement illustrates just how fundamental Berger considers Weber's influence to be, not only on his sociological theory but also on his methodology, which he outlined in particular in *Sociology Reinterpreted* (Berger & Kellner 1981). For an intellectual who mistrusts -isms as a matter of principle, it is almost tantamount to a confession:

> At my age I am no longer a champion of orthodoxies, except for Weberianism, of which I have been a devoted follower since my student days. That means that, in absolute fidelity to Max Weber, I believe in "value-free" social science. (2008a: 198; our translation)

This quotation reveals not only the dominant influence of Max Weber's understanding of science, but also the kind of legitimation pressure that Berger is under. This pressure stems from the fact that he is a social scientist who regards himself as a sociologist *and* an ethicist—to wit, a social ethicist in the literal sense of the word—and he has never forbidden himself to pronounce value judgments on social phenomena.

Berger's affinity with Max Weber was fostered by his Doktorvater Carl Mayer, who was his most important teacher at the Graduate Faculty of the New School in New York. In the preface to *Invitation to Sociology* (1963: viii), Berger pays tribute to him:

> In all my thinking on my chosen field I owe an immense debt of gratitude to my teacher Carl Mayer. If he should read this book, I suspect that there will be passages that will make him raise an eyebrow. I still hope that he would not regard the conception of sociology here presented as too much of a travesty on the one he has been conveying to his students.

His extensive reading of Weber's works had not only a methodological (cf. Chapter 5 below) but also a programmatic impact on Berger's work. Hence, he does not dispute the fact that CURA's agenda can be described as neo-Weberian (cf. Chapter 4 below). Moreover, when developing their theory for the sociology of knowledge, Berger and Luckmann took as one of their starting points Max Weber's postulate that "both for sociology in the present sense, and for history, the object of cognition is the subjective meaning-complex of action" (Weber 1978 [1922]: 13).

However, in their reformulation of the sociology of knowledge (Berger & Luckmann 1966a), the authors did not limit themselves to Max Weber's position. Rather, they integrated Weber's "marching orders for sociology" with those given by Emile Durkheim, although the two approaches had hitherto been considered to be largely incompatible. In *The Rules of Sociological Method* (1938 [1895]: 14), Durkheim states: "The first and most fundamental rule is: Consider social facts as things." The combination of these two perspectives yielded Berger and Luckmann's famous question for sociological theory:

> How is it possible that subjective meanings *become* objective facticities? Or, in terms appropriate to the afore-mentioned theoretical positions: How is it possible that human activity (*Handeln*) should produce a world of things (*choses*)? In other words, an adequate understanding of the "reality *sui generis*" of society requires an inquiry into the manner in which this reality is constructed. This inquiry, we maintain, is the task of the sociology of knowledge. (1966a: 18)

The notion that Weber and Durkheim's positions were compatible may also have been influenced by the authors' reception of Werner Stark's book *The Sociology of Knowledge: An Essay in Aid of a Deeper Understanding of the History of Ideas* (1998 [1958]). Although Stark regards "the theory of functional integration as the substantial truth in matters of social determination," he supplements it with recourse to Max Scheler and Max Weber:

> . . . for both taught that ideas came into existence under the aegis of guiding values, and values, in their very nature, are never "pure ideas" of the Platonic variety, residing in a metaphysical empyrean without reference to human affairs, but [are] always calls to a definitive mode of action as well as sources of a definite mode of thought, continually giving birth at the same time to subjective beliefs and attitudes and to objective features of life. (ibid., 272)[2]

Berger and Luckmann were introduced to Durkheim's sociology at the Graduate Faculty of the New School, especially by Albert Salomon, who convinced them of the validity of a number of Durkheim's key theses—first and foremost the insight that social facts must be considered as things, and that a society's ability to function depends on a common set of values. In *Modernity, Pluralism, and the Crisis of Meaning* (1995a: 54), a publication they coauthored many years later, Berger and Luckmann refer explicitly to Durkheim's concept of *conscience collective*, which René König (1976: 323) describes as the "essential precondition of all social life" and as an "entity that makes rules of behavior" (our translation). However, this does not imply the authors' espousal of the strongly criticized theory of collective consciousness, but rather of what Durkheim called *représentations collectives*. This term refers to the collective ideas—that is, the common beliefs, norms, and values—of a community. Nonetheless, Berger and Luckmann remained committed to methodological individualism, arguing that the sociology of knowledge must concern itself with the socially transmitted meaning that Alfred Schutz calls "knowledge"— that is, the social stock of knowledge comprising general and special knowledge. Although this social stock of knowledge is greater than the sum of the subjective stocks of knowledge, it does not constitute a collective consciousness. Even though knowledge is for the most part socially transmitted, "its emergence as meaning is, however, due also to the original processes of constitution of the individual consciousness" (Knoblauch 2005: 121; our translation).

As in Durkheim's case, Berger and Luckmann are confronted with the question of how order or stability can be ensured in a modern society that is no longer characterized by common moral foundations. They recognize a solution to this social problem in entities that mediate between society (or general rules) and individuals (or individualized reality). Durkheim calls these entities "intermediary groups"; Berger and Luckmann (1995a: 53) use the term "intermediary institutions."

And, finally, like Durkheim, Berger was also searching for inner-worldly transcendence. While Durkheim was motivated by a desire to overcome the secular crisis that ensued after the French Revolution (cf. König 1976: 335), Berger—at a time when even theology was suffused with secularizing notions—was searching in normal human experiences for phenomena that appeared to point to another reality and that could therefore be interpreted as "signals of transcendence" (Berger 1969a: 53).

However, the influence of Alfred Schutz and—mainly via Schutz— William James on Berger's thinking with regard to transcendence is also apparent. According to Schutz (Schutz & Natanson 1982: 207ff.) and James (2007 [1890]: 291), man is confronted not by one reality, but by many realities or "sub-universes." While the existence of a supernatural reality beyond the reality of everyday life constitutes Berger's main theological theme, the focus of his confrontation with modernity and individuation is on how people cope with what Alfred Schutz (loc. cit.) termed the "multiple realities" in this world. His in-depth analysis of Robert Musil's novel *The Man Without Qualities* (cf. Berger 1970b, 1998e) helped him to gain an understanding of Schutz's concept (see Chapter 2 below).

It was also Alfred Schutz who introduced Berger to phenomenology as a pre- or protosociologically necessary enterprise that serves to "clarify the foundations of knowledge in everyday life, to wit, the objectivations of subjective processes (and meanings) by which the *inter*subjective commonsense world is constructed" (Berger & Luckmann 1966a: 20). From the outset, Berger's interest in phenomenology was limited to those philosophical aspects that he deemed useful for sociological theory.[3] Luckmann, on the other hand, immersed himself much more deeply in the philosophical program of phenomenology. Berger recalls that, "Unlike others with whom I worked in the early stages of my career (notably Thomas Luckmann and Maurice Natanson), I never entered in great depth into the Husserlian universe of discourse; Alfred Schutz was my major connection with the latter, and . . . this always left me in the antechamber rather than the inner sanctuary of the phenomenological edifice" (1986d: 223).

Both Max Weber and Alfred Schutz exerted an important influence not only on Berger's sociological theory building but also on his methodological understanding. Indeed, Berger probably owes his awareness of the need for conceptual clarity to Weber and Schutz. Moreover, he recalls that Schutz's requirement that PhD exam candidates summarize the key findings of their dissertation in three sentences at the beginning of their doctoral examination was instrumental in encouraging him to express his thoughts with clarity and brevity.

In connection with their reception of symbolic interactionism, Berger and Luckmann (1966a: 193–94, Note 25) explicitly refer to Friedrich Tenbruck, whom they credit in particular with "drawing heavily and successfully upon Mead and the Meadian tradition in the construction of sociological theory." The ideal types of the social distribution of knowledge described in *The Social Construction of Reality* are derived from Tenbruck (cf. Knoblauch 2005: 162–63). Berger's collaboration with Tenbruck originally came about via Luckmann. He kept it up while he was working on the research project at the Protestant Academy in Bad Boll. However, it fizzled out eventually because the working relationship became somewhat difficult for all concerned.

It should be clear by now that Thomas Luckmann has been Peter L. Berger's most important collaborator. As mentioned earlier, they first met at a philosophy seminar given by Karl Löwith at the New School. Berger recalls that the seminar was quite boring and that he noticed Luckmann, who was trying to keep awake by doodling. This encounter marked the beginning of a deep friendship and a productive scientific collaboration that yielded—to mention just one, albeit very successful, result—*The Social Construction of Reality* (Berger & Luckmann 1966a). Writing about this collaboration, Luckmann (2001: 17–18) recalls the "breathtaking speed with which Berger hammered away at the type-writer, when, in the grip of inspiration, he put to paper a formulation to be used in one of our joint texts." Most importantly, however, this collaboration was marked by great synchrony and harmony. Both men share not only a common mother tongue, experience of emigration, enthusiasm for the Habsburg—*k.u.k*—monarchy, and an affinity with certain philosophical and scientific traditions but also a fundamental consensus. In his laudatory speech on the occasion of the award of the Paul Watzlawick Ring of Honor to Berger in Vienna in 2008, Luckmann stated succinctly, "In other words whatever, or whoever, he found stupid, I found stupid, and vice versa. It must have been a pre-scientific elective affinity that stemmed from our different, but at the same time common, Kakanian roots."

While it was Berger, a confessed Protestant with a long-standing interest in philosophical questions, who got Luckmann, a confessed Catholic, interested in the sociology of religion (Berger & Luckmann 1963d, 1966c), it was Luckmann who fostered Berger's receptiveness to phenomenology and the problems of identity (Berger & Luckmann 1964b, 1966b). The two men later went separate ways in the sociology of religion insofar as their names now stand for two distinctly different concepts of religion (cf. Chapter 3 below). That this dissent did not undermine their consensus on other matters is illustrated, for example, by the fact that almost thirty years after *The Social Construction of Reality* (1966a) they coauthored quite an abstract study on *Modernity, Pluralism, and the Crisis of Meaning* (1995a), which was commissioned by the Bertelsmann Foundation. As in the case of *The Limits of Social Cohesion* (1997b), it was submitted as a report to the Club of Rome.

The *Limits of Social Cohesion* was a study of eleven countries with normative or political conflicts. The project was directed by Berger; both Luckmann and Hansfried Kellner were involved in an advisory capacity. Kellner was also a member of what Berger (2011: 80–81) jestingly calls the "clique" that came up with the idea for *The Sociological Construction of Reality* (1966a). In the end, that project was realized by Berger and Luckmann only, as the other members of the group—Kellner, Maurice Natanson, and Stanley Pullberg—were occupied with other projects.[4] Berger collaborated with Kellner on an article entitled "Marriage and the Construction of Reality. An Exercise in the Microsociology of Knowledge" (1964). In retrospect, this is quite amusing because Berger was married to Kellner's sister.[5] The collaboration with Kellner, which was strengthened—or, at least, not weakened—by their family ties, also yielded *Sociology Reinterpreted. An Essay on Method and Vocation* (Berger & Kellner 1981). The book was a statement of their understanding of sociology, and, as evidenced by its explicitly exhortative character (". . . what sociologists do, . . . what they are, . . . and what they *should* do and be" [ibid., 2]), it was addressed to sociologists in the making.

Berger's wife Brigitte participated in the conversations of the clique, many of which took place in Mexico, where the Berger family spent the summer months between 1969 and 1972 at the invitation of Ivan Illich. As mentioned earlier, Illich ran a think tank called the Centro Intercultural de Documentación ("Intercultural Documentation Center") in Cuernavaca. Influenced by their discussions with Illich about Latin America's development problems, the Bergers and Hansfried Kellner started working on *The Homeless Mind: Modernization and Consciousness* (1973a) while in Mexico. Despite the fact that the two men held increasingly opposing views, Illich strongly impressed Berger, who admired the fact that he had formed his opinions independently of any ideological camp.

In 1972, Peter and Brigitte Berger published a textbook entitled *Sociology: A Biographical Approach,* in which basic sociological phenomena were presented in the order in which they would be encountered in the course of an individual biography. Some ten years later, the Bergers coauthored *The War over the Family: Capturing the Middle Ground* (1983a). The book provoked fierce controversy—not only in the doctrinaire feminist milieu in which Brigitte Berger had unwittingly, and unwillingly, landed when she took up the post of sociology chairman at Wellesley College in 1979, but also in conservative circles (cf. Berger 2011: 155).

Berger's close friendship with Richard Neuhaus, a Lutheran minister who later converted to Catholicism, was of great importance when it came to analyzing theological and religious issues. What the two men had in common was their critical attitude toward the Protestant church that prompted them to initiate the Hartford Appeal for Theological Affirmation (cf. 1976a). What divided them was the fact that, when Neuhaus converted to Catholicism, he could not understand why Berger did not display the same religious rigor and follow suit.

When he founded the Institute for the Study of Economic Culture (ISEC) at Boston University in 1985, Berger extended the scope of his collaborations internationally and interdisciplinarily. His modus operandi as director of ISEC (and its reincarnations IRWA and CURA) was to have the field research for the institute's projects conducted and coordinated by recognized experts on the research topic in question (see Chapter 4 below). This gave rise to a network in which several members were integrated on a permanent basis. These members included, for example, David Martin, an expert on Pentecostalism in Latin America; Ann Bernstein, an expert on the situation in South Africa; Bob Weller, who specialized in developments in Southeast Asia; Grace Davie, an expert on European secularization; and the Islam expert Robert Hefner, who later succeeded Berger as director of the Institute on Culture, Religion and World Affairs (CURA). Moreover, Berger cooperated on a one-off basis with other scholars, for example Samuel Huntington, with whom he codirected the project that yielded *Many Globalizations* (Berger & Huntington 2002a).

The list of Berger's main academic collaborators would not be complete without Anton Zijderveld, a scholar who came from theology to sociology, and who holds doctoral degrees in both sociology and philosophy. As mentioned earlier, Berger has a dislike of all collectives—including intellectual "schools." And, by his own account, he did not gear his academic career toward the formation of such a school. Hence, he would not himself describe Zijderveld as his pupil. However, Zijderveld explicitly dedicated his book *The Abstract Society* (1970: ix) to "two of his teachers . . . Hans C. Hoekendijk and Peter L. Berger." In the preface to the book, Zijderveld notes, "I had been initiated in the basic principles of empirical sociology before I met him [Berger, MP], but it was only after I worked with him as a teaching assistant that the demon of sociological inquisitiveness took hold of me" (ibid., x). In the 1970s, Berger and Zijderveld's common focus was the analysis of modern society and modern consciousness. Nowadays, however, their collaboration is grounded in their interest in philosophical questions—which yielded *In Praise of Doubt,* a book they authored jointly in 2009. Berger asked Zijderveld to be his coauthor "because he wanted to work on this topic with someone who had greater philosophical expertise" (2009: vii).

Berger's bibliography impressively documents the fact that, for him, scholarly work means collaboration—also when it comes to publishing. However, it would appear that the numerous collaborations he has entered into in the course of his working life have been motivated by several different factors. In many cases, they represent a meaningful division of labor—as a remedy for the hubris of sole authority and

8

general expertise, as it were. However, they have sometimes served to produce what Berger (1983b: 243), with reference to Musil's *The Man without Qualities* (1995 [1930ff.]), calls a "plausibility structure"—in other words, "social relationships that serve to stabilize and support his reality" (our translation).

Notes

1. Theological influences on Berger's sociology of knowledge will not be dealt with here because they are neither readily recognizable nor does Berger himself deem them to be of relevance.

2. Although Stark "earths" values to a certain extent here, his sociology of knowledge is nonetheless based on a positivistic notion of knowledge, which is problematic from the perspective of Berger and Luckmann's sociology of knowledge (cf. Knoblauch 2005: 113).

3. A remark in the preface to *Redeeming Laughter* (1997a) is illustrative of Berger's understanding of phenomenology: "The book begins naively (or, which is more or less the same thing, phenomenologically) by just *looking at* the experience of the comic as it appears in ordinary life, without recourse to any academic disciplines."

4. Maurice Natanson, whom Berger describes as a brilliant phenomenologist, went on to become a professor of philosophy at Yale University. Berger coauthored the essay "Reification and the Sociological Critique of Consciousness" (1965e) with Stanley Pullberg.

5. This fact gives added meaning to Jean-Claude Kaufmann's deliberations on the content of this microsociology of knowledge: "Couples frequently talk a lot—and about lots of things. Most of these conversations appear at first glance to be trivial chatter. However, Peter L. Berger and Hansfried Kellner . . . demonstrate that this is by no means the case, and that [these conversations] play an important role. They are the instrument that enables [the couple] to construct a common perspective and a common reality day after day and to feel reinforced in their various perceptions because they listen to each other and speak with the same voice. Conversation is the prerequisite to their life together" (Kaufmann 1994: 226; our translation).

Reflections on the Twenty-Fifth Anniversary of *The Social Construction of Reality*

by Peter L. Berger

A number of times during recent years I have come across references to this book as a "classic" (sometimes, in a more humbling mode, as a "*minor* classic"). This is, of course, very gratifying, as was Chris Prendergast's generous invitation to contribute these reflections.[1] As with most gratifications in this life, there is a disturbing downside. The author of a "classic" (even a minor one) is commonly assumed to be deceased or soon to be so, which is a condition to which I do not as yet aspire. Be this as it may, I will do my best to rise (no pun intended) to the occasion.

When Thomas Luckmann and I decided to write this book, in the early 1960s, our intentions were quite modest. We were both junior members of the Graduate Faculty of the New School for Social Research, our common *alma mater* to which we had returned after some years of teaching elsewhere. We found ourselves in the lucky situation of being in the company of a small but lively group of young colleagues and graduate students who broadly shared a theoretical orientation, the one that all of us had learned from our teacher Alfred Schutz. One of Schutz's unrealized projects had been to formulate a new theoretical foundation for the sociology of knowledge in terms of his blend of phenomenology and Weberian theory. We intended to realize this project. It was only in the course of working on the book that we discovered, to our own surprise, that the project developed a more ambitious scope. A broad theoretical paradigm for doing

11

sociology seemed to take shape under our hands. This excited and pleased us, but, although we were young enough for any amount of *chutzpah,* we did not expect that many other people would share our excitement. We were conscious of our marginality in relation to the American sociological enterprise and we did not anticipate the changes that were about to occur in the field (changes, as it turned out, which did not make us any less marginal). When the book was finished, however, we were very happy with the result. Nothing that has happened since then has made us change our minds. Both of us, as we recently decided once again, would change very little in the book if we were to rewrite it today, and both of us have found its theoretical paradigm eminently useful as we turned our attention to a number of different areas of empirical inquiry.

One question asked by the editor in his letter of invitation was, "Did you mean to found a school of social theory, in which case why did you decline to lead it?" I have already answered the first part of the question; as to the second part, one can only decline an offer that has been made. No one offered. Even if one allows that the paradigm proposed by us might have formed the basis of a "school," the failure of such a development is not difficult to explain. There is, of course, the obvious fact that we were situated in an emphatically peripheral, non-elite institution. But even if we had been on the faculty of, say, Harvard or Columbia (a fate I would not necessarily wish on either one of us), I'm not at all sure that the history of these ideas would have been very different. The book was published and attracted widespread attention during what, as is now clear, was a very narrow window of opportunity for a reconstruction of sociology. In 1966, when the book came out, there was broad dissatisfaction with what had been the long hegemony of structural-functionalism in theory and a narrow positivism in the day-to-day practice of most sociologists. Especially younger people in the discipline were looking for something new, something that would transcend the aridity of both Parsonian scholasticism and the endless refinements of quantitative techniques. Something new was indeed about to engulf sociology, but it was not the marriage of Weber and Schutz celebrated in *The Social Construction of Reality.* It was, of course, the orgy of ideology and utopianism that erupted all over the academic scene in the late 1960s, almost immediately after the publication of our book. Neither Luckmann nor I had any sympathy with this *Zeitgeist,* but even if we had been more sympathetic, our sort of sociology was not what all these putative revolutionaries were clamoring for. It is not possible to play chamber music at a rock festival.

The collaboration between Luckmann (who remains one of my closest friends) and me ended for the very simple reason that he accepted a position in Europe; it is possible to collaborate on empirical studies across oceans, but joint work in theory requires (to mix a Weberian and Schutzian phrase) the *pianissimo* of the face-to-face situation. Luckmann must speak for himself on how be sees his relationship to the organized discipline, but I have long reconciled myself to my marginality with respect to the American sociological establishment (which, though perhaps I have missed something, does not seem to me more congenial than it was two decades ago). Although I have continued to do sociology, I have done so in an increasingly interdisciplinary context, a situation in which I feel very comfortable.

Not long after our little group in New York dispersed in all directions, and for reasons that had nothing to do with this, I became interested in problems of modernization and Third World development, and these problems have remained my major intellectual focus ever since. The paradigm that we developed in *Social Construction* has shown itself to be eminently applicable. Modernization can only be understood if one perceives it as a phenomenon both of institutional change and of transformations of consciousness, and it is precisely this duality that the paradigm was meant to deal with. Obviously this is not the place to demonstrate this claim, so I can only affirm my satisfaction that this theoretical orientation has shown itself, time and again, to be useful in illuminating concrete empirical discipline. Since 1985 I have directed the Institute for the Study of Economic Culture at Boston University, which now brings together a singularly stimulating and productive team of young social scientists. Sociologists are in a distinct minority in this group, and the last thing on earth the Institute seeks to do is to propagate some sort of sociology-of-knowledge orthodoxy. But the very concept of "economic culture," denoting the interface between economic institutions and various elements of culture (ideas, religion, morality, lifestyles), lends itself beautifully to elaborations in terms of the sociology of knowledge. Whether one looks at cultural aspects of the "economic miracles" of East Asia; the socioeconomic consequences of the rapid growth of Protestantism in Latin America or the way in which themes from the counterculture have been absorbed into corporate life in the United States (all topics of current Institute studies); one must find a way of relating events within institutional structures to movements within the consciousness of individuals. I, for one, have not found a better guide to doing this than the one Luckmann and I first cooked up during many interminable conversations all these many years ago.

I have been extraordinarily busy pursuing my own intellectual agenda and I have not paid much attention to the currents of thought that, in recent years, have taken or been given the label "constructivist." What I have come across under this designation has not exactly evoked sentiments of kinship rediscovered. Again, I may have missed something, but the "constructivist" literature that I have seen seems to come from the aforementioned ideological cauldron with which I have no affinity whatever. The notion of the social construction of reality is here reinterpreted in neo-Marxist, or "critical," or "post-structuralist" terms, and it is radically altered in this translation. It is one thing to say that all social reality is interpreted reality (which is what Luckmann and I said in all our various propositions); it is an altogether different thing either to say that there are privileged interpreters or, on the contrary, to say that all interpretations are equally valid. Hansfried Kellner and I tried to formulate our understanding of the act of interpretation in our little book *Sociology Reinterpreted* (1981), but I'm not aware of any great impact of our formulation. As to ethnomethodology, I have been very much impressed by some of the early work of the school, especially that of Harold Garfinkel, though it seems to me that it owes as much to Chicago-type American sociology as to Schutz. I have not kept up with what seems to be the increasingly esoteric direction taken by a number of ethnomethodologists more recently. In any case, the major if not the only empirical application of this approach has been microsociological; by contrast, my interests have developed in an increasingly macrosociological direction, and I don't think that ethnomethodology can be very helpful there.

Finally, the editor asks whether I have any message for social theorists. I don't really consider myself as someone called to issue messages to the world (a missionary role that requires, I think, an absence of any sense of the comic), not even to that minute and not terribly important part of the world inhabited by social theorists. But I suppose that I do have a message of sorts.

Social theory, and indeed the discipline of sociology as such, originated in the effort to grasp intellectually the cataclysmic transformation that we now call modernization. Sociology in particular came out of minds struggling with the "big questions" of the modern age. Sociology entered a period of decline when it bifurcated into two groups, those who saw the discipline as an instrument of agitation and propaganda, and those who saw it as a technical tool kit (some individuals, a wonder to behold, managed to belong to *both* groups). In other works, some sociologists only looked at questions to which they already believed to have the answers and others only looked at those questions that could be answered by means of very narrowly conceived methods. In consequence, sociology today subsists under the twin distortions of ideology on the one hand and triviality on the other. Not surprisingly, the status of the discipline has gone into a steep decline. I would think that this decline will continue, possibly to the point of extinction, unless these two distortions are overcome. If I have a message, then, it would be to return to the "big questions," of which, God knows, there is no scarcity in the world today. I must leave it to others to pass judgment on the "classic" (or "*minor* classic") quality of *The Social Construction of Reality.* But to those who want to deal with the monumental realities of our moment in history without ideological blinders, messianic pretensions or methodological rigidity, I would suggest that a theoretical blending of Max Weber and Alfred Schutz will still serve them quite well.

Note

1. This article appeared in "Perspectives," the Theory Section newsletter of the American Sociological Association, Vol. 15, No. 2, April 1992.

2

Modernity and Pluralism

One of the first fruits of Peter L. Berger's analytical confrontation with modernity was *The Homeless Mind* (Berger, Berger, & Kellner 1973a), a book he coauthored with his wife Brigitte and his brother-in-law, Hansfried Kellner. The book—and Berger's interest in modernity—have a biographical history: "The ideas in it began to germinate during 1969, when one of the authors [Peter L. Berger, MP] (for political rather than scholarly reasons) became seriously interested in the problems of 'development' in Latin America" (ibid., 8).[1] One reason for this interest was Berger's encounter with Ivan Illich, who, as mentioned earlier, had started a think tank in Mexico in the early 1960s, most of whose members were Marxists. One of the main concerns of these Marxist scholars was the critical confrontation with modernization theories produced by North American social scientists. They rejected these theories as developmentalism (*desarrollismo*), in the pejorative sense of the word, and decried them as development ideology.

The main intention of *The Homeless Mind* (1973a) was to confront what the authors deemed to be an oversimplified Marxist analysis of the development problems in Latin America (and Africa) with a more complex interpretation. From the Marxist perspective, capitalism is the root of all evil; it explains not only the peculiarity of modern institutions but also the peculiarity of modern consciousness, which Marxist theory debunks as "false consciousness." The authors' desire to engage with Marxist notions about development explains the general thrust of the book.

Basically, *The Homeless Mind* contrasts institutional processes and consciousness structures in advanced industrial societies (the First World) with those of less modernized societies in Asia, Africa, and Latin America (the Third World). However, as Justin Stagl (2001) points out, the Second World is not dealt with at all, nor is the thematic complex of capitalism/socialism as a whole. Berger (2001a: 168) concedes that this criticism is justified:

> Almost without exception all our scientific interlocutors were Marxists. We wanted to make it clear to them that, even without capitalism and within the socialist systems they desired, technology and bureaucracy must inevitably lead to modern consciousness structures—including the "alienation" (in our terminology "homelessness") they so deplored. That made sense at the time but it distorted our analysis.

He later remedied this distortion, first in *Pyramids of Sacrifice* (1974a) and, even more so, in *The Capitalist Revolution* (1986a) (see Chapter 3 below).

The contribution that *The Homeless Mind* (1973a) makes to the sociology of knowledge is grounded in the authors' insight that their line of argument called for a much more comprehensive and in-depth analysis of modern consciousness per se, and that this analysis required a solid sociology-of-knowledge foundation. They arrived at this insight only in the course of their analysis of the processes of consciousness that accompanied and, in turn, impacted the modernization of what was known at the time as the Third World.[2] In their analysis of the malaise resulting from the homelessness—or, as it was then called, alienation—that is considered to be symptomatic of the way in which modern man experiences the world, the authors concretize the dialectical relationship between objective givenness and subjective meaning that had been abstractly formulated in *The Social Construction of Reality* (Berger & Luckmann 1966a). This relationship manifests itself empirically in the world of institutions, which confronts the modern *individual* as external reality, and in the consciousness structures intrinsic in that social reality.

In *The Homeless Mind* (1973a: 20–21), the authors develop a comprehensive conceptual apparatus for their sociology-of-knowledge analysis of modernity. Key components are:

a) the distinction between the organization of knowledge and cognitive style—that is, between the what and the how of conscious experience; these structures of consciousness are located in a general frame of reference (horizon) and are embedded in a symbolic universe;

b) the distinction between institutions, or institutional processes, as primary or secondary carriers of modernization; these carriers are the social basis for specific structures of consciousness that the authors call plausibility structures;[3] and

c) the distinction between intrinsically necessary *packages* of modernity that cannot be taken apart if the modernization process is to continue, and extrinsic packages that have come about by historical accident and can be more readily taken apart and reassembled without halting that process. The *package* concept, which is derived from Ivan Illich, is understood as "an empirically given combination of institutional process and clusters of consciousness" (ibid., 21).

In *The Homeless Mind* (1973a), Berger and his coauthors also remain faithful to the second basic principle articulated in *The Social Construction of Reality* (Berger & Luckmann 1966a: 15), namely that the sociology of knowledge must concern itself primarily with commonsense knowledge rather than with theoretical thought and ideas, and with ordinary people rather than intellectuals: "A sociology of knowledge that understands itself in terms of the analysis of everyday consciousness would be ill-advised to concentrate on this small number of intellectuals" (1973a: 29). Therefore, in the first step of their analysis, the authors concentrate on the consciousness of "an ordinary worker in contemporary industry" rather than on engineers and scientists (1973a: 30). In the second step, instead of focusing on the consciousness of bureaucrats, they concern themselves with the "typical client of an agency of political bureaucracy" (ibid., 45).

Inherent in the assumption of a dialectic between external and internal conditions is the problem of infinite regress. In other words, the analysis must arbitrarily begin at one point and therefore can never represent reality in its totality. Because the authors are specifically interested in the way modern consciousness evolves, their analysis takes as its starting point the institutional prerequisites of modernization, namely technology and bureaucracy. However, they fail to analyze the antecedent processes on the level of individual consciousness and the way in which modern consciousness impacts, or acts back upon, these institutions. They are aware that this is problematic, which is why they stress that their approach should not be misconstrued as mono-causal or deterministic. Indeed, they acknowledge the likelihood that:

> . . . the great transformation could not have taken place without antecedent processes that were neither technological nor economic (as, for example, religious and ethical interpretations of the world). Nor do we assume such one-sided causation in the contemporary situation. While we believe that the underlying "engine" of modernization is technological/economic, we are fully aware of the

19

multiplicity of forces *acting back* upon this "engine," and, let it be added, we do not claim to be able to provide a comprehensive theory ordering all these forces in some neat parallelogram. (1973a: 16)

2.1 Modernization

"Modernization implies the radical transformation of all external conditions of human existence" (Berger & Luckmann 1995a: 44). The material extent of this transformation is particularly evident when one calls to mind the living conditions in premodern times. The French historian and novelist Zoé Oldenbourg did so in her novel *Argile et Cendres* (1979 [1946]; English title: *The World is Not Enough*), which tells the life story of an aristocratic couple in twelfth-century France. In his lectures, Peter L. Berger has often used this story for comparison purposes. After her arranged marriage at the age of fourteen to Ansiau, the sixteen-year-old son of a minor baron, Alis, the central female protagonist, bears a child every year. All her offspring, save two or three, die in infancy. For Alis's aristocratic husband, who is away on crusade most of the time, the children are of little importance. However, she at least remembers the names of her many children buried in the graveyard behind the castle. Both spouses pass away at what was then the grand old age of forty.

What struck Berger on his first trips to developing countries, especially Brazil and Mexico, was the fact that living conditions such as this persisted almost unchanged—at least as far as infant mortality was concerned. Herein lay his basic dissent with Ivan Illich, a man whom he held in great esteem. In contrast to Illich, who was an ardent critic of modernization, Berger was convinced that all those developments that provoke a feeling of psychological homelessness are nothing compared to the existentially threatening living conditions in premodern times, under which, as Zoé Oldenbourg's novel shows, even the upper classes suffered. Berger's moral verdict is that modernization cannot be cancelled or reversed, as Illich, Gandhi, and even Tolstoy had romantically postulated.

In *Pyramids of Sacrifice* (1974a), in particular, Berger explores how political ethics can be applied to social change without succumbing either to capitalist ideology, which is founded upon "the myth of growth," or to socialist ideology, which is based on "the myth of revolution." Berger places his hopes in institutional arrangements that neither ignore nor annihilate opposition against modernization, but rather take it duly into account. By "bringing together scientific analysis and ethical concern" (1974a: 7), Berger deliberately steps outside the boundaries of value-free scientific analysis within which *The Homeless Mind* (1973a) is located.

In the latter book, Berger, Berger, and Kellner analyze the consciousness-shaping force of the fundamental engines of modernization, namely scientifically based technological production and—secondary thereto—the bureaucratic state. They identify as the principal cause of modernization the "transformation of the world by technology" (ibid., 15).[4] The authors do not claim that this insight is original. Rather, they acknowledge that Thorstein Veblen recognized earlier and more astutely than other sociologists that technology was the engine and engineers the central protagonists of the process of modernization. However, they consider that Veblen over-glorified engineers as heroes of modernity.

Berger et al. focus on the "institutional concomitants of technologically induced economic growth" (ibid., 15). Following Weberian usage, they differentiate between primary and secondary carriers of modernization. The former comprise the institutions of technological production and bureaucracy; the latter include institutional processes such as urbanization, mass media, and mass education. The authors understand modernization as "the growth and diffusion of a set of institutions rooted in the transformation of the economy by means of technology" (loc. cit.).

Berger et al. assume the existence of "reciprocal relations of causality"—in the Weberian sense of elective affinity—between these institutional processes and processes on the level of consciousness (loc. cit.). Accordingly, certain transformations of consciousness go hand in hand with institutional processes that emerge at certain historical points. Once established, these processes act back upon individual consciousness. In his seminal work *The Protestant Ethic and the Spirit of Modern Capitalism* (2003[1904/05]), Max Weber identifies the constellation of values and attitudes that he deems to be the *conditio sine qua non* of modern capitalism. For their part, Berger et al. (1973a: 102–105) identify the themes that the primary carriers—technological production and bureaucracy—contributed to modern consciousness. Together, these themes make up the symbolic universe of modernity. According to the authors, the following themes are intrinsically linked to the institutions of technological production: functional rationality, componentiality, multi-relationality, "makeability," plurality, and pro-gressivity. By contrast, the themes that are intrinsically derived from bureaucracy are: society as a subject of inquiry in itself; the phenom-enon of bureaucracy and its taxonomic actions "as a way of mitigating the threats of plurality"; the allocation of particular jurisdictional space to the private sphere; and the notion that human rights are related to bureaucratically identifiable rights. This list of bureaucracy-related themes can be supplemented by further factors that were historically operative during the modernization process in Europe and North America, but which must not inevitably occur.

The cognitive style pertaining to technological production pen-etrates the consciousness of modern man mainly via the world of work, and thereby enters the private sphere. A characteristic ele-ment of this cognitive style is the aforementioned *componentiality* of modern consciousness (ibid., 32, 102). Reality is not apprehended as forming a single entity but rather in terms of many small, discrete components that can be assembled in different ways. No longer restricted to the world of work, this perception of reality increasingly shapes social life and identity—although it finds itself in competition with the intra-subjective experience of wholeness and uniqueness. Berger et al. (ibid., 38, 211) consider the ability to experience the self to be a precondition of what Erving Goffman calls "role distance"—in other words, the establishment of subjective distance vis-à-vis certain components of one's identity.

Institutional processes such as urbanization, literacy programs, and the spread of mass communication are major agencies for the transmission of modern consciousness—that is, for the diffusion of the componential cognitive style beyond the world of work and the minds of those workers directly engaged in technological production. This can be illustrated by an attitude that the authors refer to as "make-ability," which they define as an approach to reality that is grounded in a specific type of fantasy, namely *problem-solving inventiveness* and a *general tinkering attitude* (ibid., 34). Originally a characteristic specific to an engineering or technological mentality, this attitude spreads to other sectors of life, to social experience, and to identity in general, which are then regarded as permanent problem-solving enterprises. Opposition against this notion of makeability is nourished not least by the fact that its transferability is subject to limitations. As the authors point out:

> It is possible, for example, for the individual to look upon his own psychic life in the same problem-solving and tinkering attitude with which an engineer contemplates the working of a machine. However, while the engineer has a well-tested repertoire of tinkering procedures available to him for the solving of problems in the manipulation of machines, such a repertoire is sadly underdeveloped when it comes to solving problems of the human psyche. (ibid., 35)

Although this problem-solving and tinkering attitude is frequently dismissed as delusional, failure to acknowledge it as an integral part of modern consciousness would be tantamount to throwing the baby out with the bath water.

Technological production, and the many technological alternatives associated with it, leads to the multiplication of options. This first affects the material level—not only in the form of consumption opportunities but also of diverse manufacturing and processing variants. It subsequently extends socially and intellectually to the formation of identity, biography, and lifestyle, thereby increasing choices and decision-making options. More and more aspects of human existence are no longer matters of fate. However, this also means that fewer things can be taken for granted. This leads to what Berger calls the "heretical imperative":[5]

> *In premodern situations there is a world of religious certainty, occasionally ruptured by heretical deviations. By contrast, the modern situation is a world of religious uncertainty, occasionally staved off by more or less precarious constructions of religious affirmation. . . . For premodern man, heresy is a possibility—usually a rather remote one; for modern man, heresy typically becomes a necessity. . . . modernity creates a situation in which picking and choosing becomes an imperative.* (1979: 25; emphasis in the original)

However, this new freedom of choice cannot compensate for the feeling of psychological homelessness and the accompanying malaise evoked in advanced industrial societies by the segmentation not only of personality—into work roles and private roles—but also of society—into different spheres with specific, and often conflicting, value systems. Released from a world of fate into a world of multiple options, premodern man becomes a "very nervous Prometheus" (1979: x). According to the authors of *The Homeless Mind* (Berger et al. 1973a), this is especially the case in the less modernized societies of the Third World, in which modernization, with all its implications, is imported, imposed, or driven by forces located on the periphery of society. Hence the inevitability of opposition against modernization in the form of counter-modernization or demodernization tendencies, which are manifest, for example, in counter-cultures (on "demodernizing consciousness," cf. Berger, Berger, & Kellner 1973b).

Distinguishing it explicitly from Anton Zijderveld's (1970) diagnosis of the abstract society, Berger et al. (1973a: 221) point out the limitations of anti-institutionalism: "Generally speaking, social institutions are more resilient than they appear to be during periods of transition and crisis. This is particularly true of the technological and bureaucratic institutions of a modern society." The authors assert that counter-, youth-, and subcultures are "parasitical upon the structures of modernity" to the extent that they are tolerated and subsidized by mainstream society (ibid., 222). The confidence in the resilience and efficacy of institutions, which is a recurring theme in Berger's works, stems from the reception of Arnold Gehlen's anthropological theory of institutions. In an article that they coauthored in 1965, Berger and Kellner outline Gehlen's theory:

> Man, finding himself in a state of rupture with his own biological constitution, must stabilize and specialize his activity through structures produced by himself. He must construct his own world. This world, which is culture, must aim at the firm structures which are lacking biologically. To be sure, these man-made structures can never be as firm as those of the animal world. They must be continuously produced and re-produced in human activity. As a result, they are inherently precarious and predestined to change. Social institutions are the core of this process of cultural stabilization. They are the culturally produced forms by which human activity is given coherence and continuity. (1965c: 111–12)

In other words, man's basic constitution is such that institutions that serve to stabilize culture and give human action coherence and continuity are continuously being created, legitimated, and restored.[6]

2.2 Pluralism

Even though pluralism must be regarded as a consequence of modernity, *plurality* is not exclusive to modern societies. However, as Berger and Luckmann (1995a: 29) point out, what characterizes the specific form of pluralism that comes to full fruition in modern societies is the fact that "value systems and stocks of meaning are no longer the property of all members of society." In other words, it can no longer be taken for granted that the superordinate system of meaning into which an individual is socialized is the meaning system of his contemporaries (loc. cit.).

Modernity not only engenders pluralism. Due to a whole series of structural factors, it also brings about the quantitative and qualitative reinforcement of this trend. Demographically speaking, population growth and migration—and the ensuing far-reaching urbanization—act as an intensifier, because they bring together more and more people of different origin in an increasingly dense space. This is encouraged economically by the geographic and social mobility that accompanies the market economy and industrialization. Moreover, the rule of law and democracy act as institutional guarantors of a more or less peaceful coexistence. And, finally, media- and mass communication constantly highlight the plurality of lifestyles and mentalities.

In *The Homeless Mind* (Berger et al. 1973a), pluralism is dealt with in terms of the plurality of the social life-worlds in which individuals in modern societies typically live.[7] The effects of this constellation can be clearly illustrated by long-range life planning. The authors analyze this phenomenon in terms of the organization of knowledge (for example, knowledge about the experts who may be of assistance in the planning process), cognitive style (for example, "multi-relationality") and its important implications for modern identity (ibid., 70–71, 102).

Identity problems—one of Luckmann's key themes—are also addressed by Berger, especially in his early works. In "Social Mobility and Personal Identity" (1964b), a paper that Berger and Luckmann coauthored back in 1964, they explore the effects of modern class structure and upward and downward mobility on personal identity. In this paper, which discusses the possibility of an identity crisis being caused by status inconsistencies and uncertainties, a vague outline of a theory of modern society is already visible. However, the authors focus on functional differentiation and the emergence of the private sphere; as yet, no mention is made of technology as the starting point of the modernization process. In the public sphere, individuals are of interest to society only as the bearers of functionary roles. The individual is "forced to define himself as an anonymous performer, as a 'cog in the machine'" of primary institutions. In the area of private life, by contrast, individuals are more or less left to their own devices to discover an essential identity with the help of secondary institutions that are geared to their personal choices (ibid., 336):

> The paradox of total conformity in one sector of individual existence and seemingly absolute autonomy in the other, therefore, has its roots in total performance control by the primary institutional domains combined with their indifference to the person. . . . Compared with other historical situations this leads to an underdefinition of identity.

Because neither the public sphere nor the area of private life contributes to the formation of the "highly profiled identities so characteristic of other historical periods," an "identity market supplied by secondary institutions" arises in response to the need for "essential identities" (ibid., 337).

Berger and Luckmann (ibid., 339) apprehend the spread of a quasireligious mobility ethos throughout American society (and not only there). They liken this ethos to a secularized version of intra-worldly salvation—one of the main characteristics of the Protestant ethic. In their view, the mobility ethos has the potential to become a religion in a Durkheimian sense—"that is, it can serve as an overarching integrative representation" (ibid., 340). Because of the discrepancy between this dominant mobility ethos and the objective chances of mobility, the majority of people fail to achieve their life goal: "The implication is simple: by their own definition and that of their peers . . . these individuals are failures" (loc. cit.). The most widespread pattern of adaptation used by those who fail in this way is "participation in the 'rat race' accompanied by the construction of private sanctuaries" (ibid., 341). These private sanctuaries are supposed to act as a buffer against fear of failure. But, as the authors point out, this private universe is unstable and in need of social maintenance and repair services. These services are provided by secondary institutions, for example, the churches, psychotherapy, and organized recreation (ibid., 342). However, because of their social organization and their location within a consumer culture, these secondary institutions inevitably fail in their central task of keeping the private sphere free of the mobility ethos. Instead, "they re-import the mobility ethos through the back door of a private world" (ibid., 343). Hence the modern individual cannot escape status-seeking—or the identity problems that go with it.

From a sociology-of-knowledge perspective, the domain of unquestionably certain knowledge shrinks. Individuals no longer know for sure "about the world, how to behave in it, what is reasonable to expect and, last but not least, . . . who they are" (Berger & Luckmann 1995a: 30). Under conditions of pluralism, this taken-for-granted knowledge about the world, society, life, and identity erodes. All these domains can now be interpreted in a multitude of ways, and each interpretation defines its own perspectives of possible action (loc. cit.).

In *Modernity, Pluralism, and Crisis of Meaning* (Berger & Luckmann 1995a: 46), a study commissioned by the Bertelsmann Foundation, the authors use the metaphor of the coffeemaker to illustrate how these changes in consciousness come about. Those perceptions that are taken for granted lie in the depths, on the level of what (Schutz & Natanson 1982) calls "the world-taken-for-granted." The moderniza-tion of consciousness causes these perceptions to evaporate upward to the "sphere of insecurity, that which is not taken for granted, opinions which I am in principle prepared to revise or even retract." This process takes place at the expense of the solid (coffee) grounds of certainty.

The present description of the modernization process would be incomplete if one were to ignore the role of the institutions that serve as guarantors of the world-taken-for-granted. Following Berger and Luckmann (1966a: 53ff.), "institutionalization" refers to the process of sedimentation, objectivation, and transmission of habitualized actions. "Congealed" as programs of social interaction, institutions are internalized in individual consciousness during a complex process of primary and secondary socialization. These programs guide the indi-vidual in his actions and are perceived not as somebody else's meaning but as his own. Despite numerous support and control mechanisms, to which Berger and Luckmann refer in *The Social Construction of Reality* (1966a) as "primary and secondary legitimation," a certain degree of institutional erosion is inevitable in modern societies. Under conditions of pluralism, the individual is constantly confronted with alternatives for institutionally relevant roles, identities, interpretative schemes, values, and worldviews, whose taken-for-grantedness is suc-cessively undermined by the fact that the individual is now obliged to make choices.

Hence, as Berger and Luckmann (1995a: 38–39) point out, pluralism leads to the profound relativization or, as the authors put it, "decanon-ization," of existing systems of values and schemes of interpretation. Pluralism also has a strongly relativizing effect on all worldviews; it acts like a "great relativizing cauldron" (1979: 9). This engenders "insecurity of meaning and uncertainty in moral justification" (1995a: 66), not—as is often alleged in discourse on crises of meaning and lack of orientation in modernity—because superordinate systems of values and interpretation are no longer available, but rather because there is a "multiplicity of moralities distributed across different communities of life and faith" (loc. cit.).

This multiplicity of moralities results in subjective, intersubjective, and structural crises of meaning. However, Berger and Luckmann (1995a: 39) argue that, for most members of society, at least, the diagnosis of existential disorientation, alienation, and anomie common in social and cultural criticism, is exaggerated. In the normal case—that is, under conditions of economic prosperity and in the absence of external threat—and contrary to Durkheim's assumption, social stability is maintained by counter-tendencies, such as the legalization of the rules of social life, or formal moralization—that is, the development of systems of ethics peculiar to individual functional spheres.

In his search for a social counterbalance to crises of meaning, Berger once more places hope in institutions—or rather in a specific type of institution. In a civil-society study coauthored with Richard J. Neuhaus (1996), these entities are referred to as "intermediary institutions," or "mediating structures." In the authors' view, the dichotomization of the individual and the state is oversimplified, insofar as people do not live in a sociocultural vacuum, but rather in neighborhoods, families, churches, and voluntary associations. They argue that intermediary institutions, which, following Gehlen, they also refer to as "secondary institutions," have the potential to mediate vertically, as it were, between the individual and society, and between the big economic and political institutions and individual existence. This mediation also extends to superordinate configurations of values.

As a consequence of individualization, the status of these intermediary institutions (for example, church institutions) has become increasingly precarious: they are steadily losing their powers to impose sanctions; their members are less and less willing to commit themselves in one way or another. Hence, Berger and Luckmann (1995a: 68–69) note that the most important empirical question with regard to intermediary institutions is: "Do they really mediate, and do they mediate in both directions?" This question has been researched in numerous studies conducted under the auspices of the Institute on Culture, Religion and World Affairs (CURA) and its previous incarnations. They include, for example, *Civil Islam* (Hefner 2000), a study on the prospects for civil society in the Muslim world, and *Civil Life, Globalization and Political Change in Asia* (Weller 2005), which deals with the democratizing potential of NGOs. By contrast, *The Limits of Social Cohesion: Conflict and Mediation in Pluralist Societies* (Berger 1997b), a Bertelsmann project whose findings were published as a report to the Club of Rome, focused on "horizontal mediation—that is mediation between conflicting segments in the overall society" (ibid., 363). This project compared normative conflicts in the United States, France, Germany, Hungary, Chile, South-Africa, Turkey, Indonesia, India, Japan, and Taiwan. The cross-national comparative perspective revealed that it is naive to place overly high hopes in civil society structures. As was demonstrated in the case of Germany and Japan, groups and movements with distinctly normative positions can contribute significantly to the destabilization of social order.

2.3 Individuation

Which modernity are we living in at present? The intensive discussion of this question characterizes the current debate on modernization in Germany. "Second modernity," "reflexive modernity," and "post-modernity" are the three most prominent labels produced in this discourse. Peter L. Berger views these labels with skepticism:

> The expression "post-modern" does not appeal to me in the first place. I do not believe that we are in a post-modern situation, but rather that modernization is an ongoing process; it takes on different forms. One can, however, define "post-modern" in such a way that it is acceptable, at least in western societies, [namely] as a shift from the production of material goods to that of information and knowledge, and so on. But I tend to doubt whether these things create a completely new situation. Rather, I believe that we are in a process of progressive modernization, in which certain characteristics remain the same. One of the most important of these is individuation. I do not see any great change in that regard, except that its consequences are increasingly far-reaching. (in: Brix & Prisching 2001: 153–54; our translation)

The use of the term "individuation," as opposed to the more common concept of "individualization," sets a new focus—not only terminologically. Whereas Ulrich Beck (1983), in particular, employs the term individualization to emphasize the structural aspect of the release of the individual from traditional ligatures, individuation refers to a process that originates in the person rather than the structures. This accentuation becomes understandable when one considers the traditions of thought to which Berger refers. For him, modernization goes hand in hand with "subjectivization" as defined by Arnold Gehlen. As he notes in *The Heretical Imperative* (1979: 21):

> If answers [to the perennial human question "What can I know?," MP] are not provided objectively by his society, he [the individual, MP] is compelled to turn *inward*, toward his own subjectivity, to dredge up from there whatever certainties he can manage. This inward turn is subjectivization, a process that embraces both Descartes and the man-in-the street who is puzzled about the proper course of action in this or that area of everyday life.

Besides subjectivization, "permanent reflection" (Helmut Schelsky's term) is a typically modern characteristic, as Berger (1983b) shows in his analysis of Musil's novel *The Man Without Qualities* (1995 [1930ff.]). According to Berger's interpretation (1983b: 246), Musil portrays Ulrich, his central protagonist, as the "prototype of modern man." Both in the transition between spheres or provinces of meaning within everyday reality, and in the transition to "another condition"—which is Musil's central theme—modern man encounters multiple realities not only with an (excessive) "openness for all kinds of experience of interpretation" but also with a distinct propensity toward (excessive) "reflection upon the world and himself" (loc. cit.).

However, as the authors of *The Homeless Mind* (Berger et al. 1973a: 73ff.) point out, modern identity is not only *peculiarly differentiated* (i.e., subjectively interesting); not only *peculiarly open* (i.e., unfinished); and not only *peculiarly reflective* (i.e., questioning and rationalizing). It is also *peculiarly individuated* (i.e., characterized by an insatiable longing for individual freedom, autonomy, and self-determination). Hence, the curtailing of individual rights is now deemed to be a gross violation of basic human rights. Individual autonomy is not only a Western notion labeled "individualism," according to which an individual has "rights *apart* from his community and, if necessary against it" (Berger 1992b: 102). Individual autonomy is also an integral part of every modern experience of self.

Therefore, individuation implies disembedding, a central aspect of individualization theory that Berger addresses as a problem inherent in modernity and one that is imposed, as it were, on the Global South (as the Third World is now known). The price of liberation from traditional ligatures (not only in the Global South) is the experience of being alone in a way that would be inconceivable in traditional societies: The individual is detached from the firm solidarity of his collective existence, uncertain about the norms on which to base his existence, and also in doubt about who or what he is (cf. 1980: 36).

In *A Far Glory: The Quest of Faith in an Age of Credulity* (1992b), Berger undertakes a further analysis of Musil's novel *The Man Without Qualities* (1995 [1930ff.]). When doing so, he develops his diagnosis of the crisis of modern identity into the thesis that modern subjectivity is being undermined by the application of the scientific method to the self.[8] According to his thesis, "it becomes more and more difficult to see the self as the center of the individual's actions. Instead, these actions come to be perceived as events that happen to the individual, separate from himself, explainable in terms of both external (social) and internal (organic and psychic) causes" (1992b.: 109). The modern self is a fragmented, a plural self, a "variation wheel" (ibid., 107).[9] One of the solutions to this dilemma that Berger identifies in Musil's novel is "the religious quest for the true self, revealed in transcendence" (ibid., 122).

Notes

1. In the introduction to the book (Berger et al., 1973a: 14), the authors point out that they "prefer to use the term 'development' politically rather than scientifically—that is, in a context of value-oriented policy thinking rather than in supposedly value-free analysis." This finds expression in what they deem to be the most important question in the context of political development work, namely: "How much human suffering is acceptable to achieve certain economic goals" (ibid.,13).
2. The authors were not happy with the term "Third World." However, they decided to use it "for stylistic reasons" (1973a: 16).
3. "Put differently, any kind of consciousness is plausible only in particular social circumstances. These circumstances are what we call a plausibility structure" (Berger et al., 1973a: 21). This term, which was coined by Peter L. Berger himself, and which has become an integral part of his terminology, is very similar to Shibutani's concept of "reference group" (1955).
4. The reason why the authors consider technological development rather than the natural sciences to be the cause or the primary agent of modernization is that advances in the sciences did not have any great immediate impact on society at first. Only in the course of mechanization did they have a widespread effect.
5. It is important to note that Berger does not use the word heresy in the theological sense: "The English word 'heresy' comes from the Greek verb *hairein*, which means to 'choose'. A *hairesis* originally meant, quite simply, the taking of a choice" (1979: 24–25).
6. Berger's confidence in institutions is striking. He illustrates it with a comment made by one of his students after a lecture he gave on sociological theory: "You sure are hung up on order, aren't you?" Berger confirms that this is true; he considers that it is even true of sociology per se, which he regards as being conservative in its implications for institutional order (cf. Berger 1977a: 16).

7.   The impact of pluralism on religion is addressed by Peter L. Berger in *The Sacred Canopy* (1967) and by Thomas Luckmann in *Invisible Religion* (1967).

8.   This thesis is clearly supported by the current trend in sociology, in which praxeological and governmental approaches are particularly en vogue.

9.   The variation wheel is Berger's translation of the *Variationskreisel,* a laboratory gadget invented by Musil (Berger 1992b: 107). *Kreisel* is actually the German word for gyroscope or spinning top.

Pluralism, Protestantization, and the Voluntary Principle

by Peter L. Berger

The relation between pluralism and religion has never been unambiguous. On the one hand, as has been argued especially for the American case, pluralism in religion can encourage political pluralism and thus democracy. On the other hand, pluralism tests the limits of what religious people find tolerable in the society and thus tests their acceptance of democracy if a democratically constituted regime legislates religiously unacceptable behavior. The current furor in American churches over abortion and same-sex marriage sharply illuminates this problem. (In other words, one does not have to go to the Middle East to find cases of tension between a religious code and democracy.) Also, religious and moral pluralism raises the question of how a democratic regime can ultimately be legitimated. Again, the American case is instructive: the republic was first legitimated in Protestant terms, then in Christian terms, then in Judeo-Christian terms. We now have the interesting legitimation of a putative "Abrahamic faith" (Judeo-Christian-Muslim), which is not comforting to the adherents of nonmonotheistic traditions, not to mention the religiously unaffiliated who have long been uncomfortable with religious rhetoric of any sort in American political discourse.

The "new pluralism," of course, is the result of globalization. Almost all societies are today inevitably pluralistic. Globalization has meant an enormous increase in intercultural communication. Religion has not been immune to this process of intercontinental chatter. The present essay will look at the institutional and personal implications of globalized religion and then at the relation of these to democracy.[1]

Arguably the two most dynamic religious movements in the contemporary world are resurgent Islam and popular Protantism, the latter principally in the form of the Pentecostal movement. Both are truly global phenomena. Not only are Islamic movements interacting throughout the huge region from the Atlantic Ocean to the South China Sea, but the Muslim diaspora in Europe and North America has become a powerful presence. In England, for example, more people every week attend services in mosques than in Anglican churches. For understandable reasons, attention has focused on the most aggressive versions of this globalizing Islam, but it is moderate Muslims as well as practitioners of jihad who talk to each other on the Internet and on cell phones and who gather for both clandestine and public conferences. As to Pentecostalism, it has been spreading like wildfire through Latin America, sub-Saharan Africa, parts of east Asia, and to such unlikely groups as European gypsies and hill tribes in India. David Martin, the British sociologist who pioneered in the study of cross-national Pentecostalism, estimates that there are at least 250 million Pentecostals worldwide and possibly many more. (A crucial case is China, where we know that the movement is spreading, but which is difficult to study because it is mostly illegal and therefore underground.)[2]

However, globalizing religion is by no means limited to Islam and Protestantism. The Roman Catholic Church has always been a global institution, but globalization is profoundly altering its international profile: increasingly its areas of strength are outside its traditional European heartland, with the interesting consequence that precisely those of its features that trouble progressive Catholics in, say, the Netherlands are an attraction in the Philippines or in Africa. (The Vatican is well aware of this phenomenon, which explains many of its policies.) The Russian Orthodox Church, presiding over a strong religious revival in the post-Soviet era and enjoying the favor of the Putin government, is flexing its muscles in the Balkans and the Middle East, not to mention what the Russians call the "near abroad."

Hasidic movements with headquarters in Brooklyn, New York, are sending missionaries to Israel and to Jewish communities in Eastern Europe. The so-called Jesus Movie, a film produced by an American evangelical organization and synchronized in well over a hundred languages, is being screened by aggressive missionaries in villages throughout India, despite the outrage of pious Brahmins and the opposition of the Indian government. But Hinduism is returning the compliment. Devotees dance and chant in praise of Krishna in major American and European cities. Hindu missionary organizations (ranging from the sedate Vedanta Society to the exuberant Sai Baba movement) are busily evangelizing wherever they can. Similarly, Buddhist groups with headquarters in Japan, Taiwan, and Southeast Asia are attracting sizable numbers of converts in Western countries.

If one is to get an intellectual handle on these developments, it is important to put away a view which, despite massive evidence to the contrary, is still very widespread (not least among Christian theologians): often called the "secularization theory," this view holds that modernity brings about a decline of religion. Simply put, this view has been empirically falsified. This is not the place to enlarge upon the debates that have ranged over the secularization theory in recent years. Suffice it to say that, contrary to the theory, the contemporary world, far from being secularized, is characterized by a veritable explosion of passionate religion. (There are two exceptions to this statement—western and central Europe—and a thin but influential class of "progressive" intellectuals in most countries. Again, the reasons for these exceptions cannot be discussed here.)[3]

Modernity does not necessarily lead to a decline of religion. What it does lead to, more or less necessarily, is religious pluralism. Modern developments—mass migration and travel, urbanization, literacy, and, most important, the new technology of communication—have brought about a situation in which different religious traditions are present to each other in a historically unprecedented manner. For obvious reasons this interaction is facilitated under conditions of legally protected religious liberty. But even where governments, in various degrees, try to limit or suppress religious pluralism (as is the case in China, India, and Russia), this is difficult to do under contemporary conditions.

A personal example illustrates this: a couple of years ago I visited Buenos Aires for the first time. I had long been enamored of the writings of Borges, and I was anticipating a rather romantic encounter with the world of the tango. As my taxi left the airport, the first sight that greeted me was a huge Mormon church, with a gilded Angel Moroni sitting atop its steeple. Here was an outpost of a religion born in upstate New York, which until recently had barely spread beyond Utah and certainly not beyond the United States. Today Mormonism has been experiencing impressive growth in many countries, notably in the South Pacific and Siberia. There are now large numbers of people throughout the world whose spiritual, intellectual, and social center is Salt Lake City.

Implications of Religious Pluralism

Religious pluralism has both institutional and cognitive implications. It is important to understand both. Institutionally it means that something like a religious market is established. This does not mean that concepts of market economics can be unambiguously applied to the study of religion (as has been done, very interestingly, by Rodney Stark and other American sociologists, with the use of so-called rational choice theory).[4] But what it does mean is that religious institutions must *compete* for the allegiance of their putative clientele. This competition naturally becomes more intense under a regime of religious liberty, when the state can no longer be relied upon to fill the pews. This situation inevitably affects the behavior of religious institutions, even if their theological self-understanding is averse to such changed behavior.

The clergy (using this term broadly for the officials of religious institutions) now face a rather inconvenient fact: since their authority is no longer a social given, they must seek to reestablish it by means of *persuasion*. This gives a new social role to the laity. No longer a subject population, the laity becomes a community of consumers whose notions, however objectionable on theological grounds, must be seriously addressed.

The Roman Catholic case is paradigmatic in this respect. It is fair to say that, of all Christian churches, the Roman church has the most impressive hierarchical structure, which in many ways is at the core of its self-understanding. As far as the relevant doctrine is concerned, this has not fundamentally changed, though it has been modified by the pronouncements of the Second Vatican Council and subsequent papal encyclicals. Yet the *behavior* of the church toward its lay members has changed significantly. Some Catholics have gone so far as to describe the present time as the era of the laity in the church. This may be an exaggeration, but clearly the laity has become more assertive. The past few years have offered an impressive example of this in Boston (once called the "holy city" of American Catholicism). The archdiocese, under severe financial pressure because of the huge payments made to alleged victims of clerical sexual abuse, decided to close a number of parishes. The laypeople of the parishes rose in rebellion in a way not seen before, respectfully but firmly opposing the archbishop.

The pluralistic situation also changes the relations of religious institutions with each other. Participants in a market, religious or other, not only compete but are frequently engaged in efforts to reduce or regulate the competition. Obviously attempts are made in the educational activities of religious institutions to discourage their members from going over to competitors. For example, American Judaism has made great efforts to immunize Jews against Christian missionary activities. But competing religious institutions also negotiate with each other to regulate the competition. This helps to clarify at least some of the phenomenon known as "ecumenicity": ecumenical amity among Christian churches means, at least in part, explicit or implicit agreements not to poach on each other's territory.

Until a few decades ago such a negotiating process among American Protestant churches was known as "comity." Protestant denominations portioned out certain areas for their outreach activities, allocating a particular area to, say, the Presbyterians; the others then promised to stay out of this area. This reached a somewhat bizarre climax in Puerto Rico, where the mainline denominations divided up the entire island in this way. If you knew that someone was, say, a Presbyterian, you could guess which town he or she came from. Some evangelical Protestants did not participate in this comity, much to the annoyance of other Protestants. The term has fallen into disuse, but it is still a very significant reality and now goes beyond the Protestant fold. Mainline Protestants and Catholics do not actively proselytize each other, and neither seek to proselytize Jews. Indeed, the very word *proselytization* has acquired a pejorative meaning in American religious discourse, and those who continue to practice it are looked at askance. Thus there was an outpouring of protests when not long ago the Southern Baptist Convention (the largest evangelical denomination in the United States) announced that it would continue its program to convert Jews. Sociologically speaking, one could say that today comity is informally extended to every religious group in the United States that does not engage in blatantly illegal behavior.[5]

Religious pluralism also has important implications for the subjective consciousness of individuals. This can be stated in one sentence: religion loses its taken-for-granted status in consciousness. No society can function without some ideas and behavior patterns being taken for granted. For most of history, religion was part and parcel of what was taken for granted. Social psychology has given us a good idea of how taken-for-grantedness is maintained in consciousness: it is the result of social consensus in an individual's environment. And for most of history, most individuals lived in such environments. Pluralism undermines this sort of homogeneity. Individuals are continually confronted with others who do *not* take for granted what was so taken traditionally in their community. They must now *reflect about* the cognitive and normative assumptions of their tradition, and consequently they must *make choices.* A religion that is chosen, on whatever level of intellectual sophistication, is different from a religion that is taken for granted. It is not necessarily less passionate, nor do its doctrinal propositions necessarily change. It is not so much the *what* as the *how* of religious belief that changes. Thus modern Catholics may affirm the same doctrines and engage in the same practices as their ancestors in a traditional Catholic village. But they have decided, and must continue to decide, to so believe and behave. This makes their religion both more personal and more vulnerable. Put differently, religion is subjectivized, and religious certitude is more difficult to come by.

In one of my books I described this process as the "heretical imperative" (from the Greek word *hairesis,* which means, precisely, "choice").[6] This process occurs not only in liberal or progressive religious groups. It also occurs in the most militantly conservative groups, for there too individuals have *chosen* to be militantly conservative. In other words, there is a mountain of difference between traditional and neotraditional religion. Psychologically, the former can be very relaxed and tolerant; the latter is necessarily tense and has at least an inclination toward intolerance.

Needless to say, these developments are not unique to religion. They affect all cognitive and normative definitions of reality and their behavioral consequences. I have long argued that modernity leads to a profound change in the human condition, from *fate to choice.* Religion participates in this change. Just as modernity inevitably leads to greater individuation, so modem religion is characterized by individuals who reflect upon, modify, pick, and choose from the religious resources available to them. French sociologist Danièle Hervieu-Léger calls this phenomenon *bricolage* (loosely translatable as "tinkering," as in putting together the pieces of a Lego game); her American colleague Robert Wuthnow uses the term *patchwork religion.* The American language has a wonderfully apt term for this—"religious preference"—tellingly a term derived from the world of consumption, carrying the implication that the individual decided upon this particular religious identity and that in the future he or she might make a different decision.

Putting together the institutional and the subjective dimensions of pluralism, we can arrive at a far-reaching proposition: under conditions of pluralism all religious institutions, sooner or later, become voluntary associations—and they become so whether they like it or not.

Max Weber and Ernst Troeltsch classically analyzed two prototypical social forms of religion—the "church," into which one is born, and the "sect," which one decides to join. Richard Niebuhr suggested that American religion invented a third type, the "denomination," which he defined as a church that recognizes the right of other churches to exist, be it de jure or de facto. One could then say that, in the course of American religious history, all religious groups have become "denominationalized." Even Judaism, despite its distinctive merging of religious and ethnic identity, split into at least three denominations in America (and, depending on how one counts, several more). But the process of denominationalization is no longer limited to the United States. As pluralism spreads globally, all religious groups become in fact voluntary associations, even if they have to be dragged into this social form kicking and screaming. Not surprisingly, some of them will perceive pluralism as a lethal threat and will mobilize all available resources to resist it.

A simple conclusion follows from the preceding considerations: the capacity of a religious institution to adapt successfully to a pluralist environment will be closely linked to its capacity to take on the social form of the voluntary association. And that, of course, will be greatly influenced by its preceding history. If this is understood, then Protestantism clearly has what may be called a comparative advantage over other religious traditions (Christian or not). Both the Lutheran and the Calvinist Reformations, in their emphasis on the conscience of the individual, have an a priori affinity with modern individuation and thus with the pluralist dynamic. But not all Protestant groups have had the same capacity to organize themselves as voluntary associations.

David Martin recently suggested that three types of relations between religion and society developed in the postmedieval history of Western Christianity (the case of Eastern Orthodoxy is different).[7] The first type he calls the "baroque counter-Reformation," which sought to maintain or reestablish a harmonious unity between church, state, and society. It flourished in the *ancien régime* of Catholic Europe and, following the French Revolution, morphed into the republic understood as a sort of secular *(laique)* church. In both its sacred and secular versions, this type has great difficulties with pluralism. The second type he calls "enlightened absolutism," characteristic of Lutheran northern Europe and the Anglican establishment. It became gradually more tolerant of pluralist diversity and eventually morphed into the north European welfare state. The third type is what Martin nicely labels "the Amsterdam-London-Boston bourgeois axis," which may be seen as the matrix of religious pluralism. But, again, not all three points on this axis have been equally hospitable to voluntary association. Dutch pluralism flourished under a famously tolerant regime, but its diverse religious groups (Calvinist, Arminian, Catholic) became rather rigidly solidified as "pillars" *(verzuiling)* of an overarching political establishment. In England there occurred a more ample flourishing of diverse religious groups—the wide spectrum of so-called Nonconformity—but, as already indicated by this name, it did so under the shadow of the Anglican state church. It was in the English-speaking colonies in what became the United States that religious pluralism attained its most unconstrained and exuberant version, giving birth to the denomination as the religious voluntary association par excellence. Naturally enough, American society has ever since been the vanguard of both religious and secular pluralism.

The comparative advantage of Protestantism continues today. The amazing cross-national success of Pentecostalism and other forms of popular Protestantism can in no small measure be explained by a distinctive capacity to operate as voluntary associations. But a religious group need not be Protestant to be able to reorganize itself denominationally, even if, so to speak, it does help to be Protestant. I have already mentioned post–Vatican II Catholicism and American Judaism as cases in point. Other cases can be found far from the Judeo-Christian world. The upsurge of Buddhist and other religious movements in Japan since the 1950s (one author calls it "the rush hour of the gods")[8] has been largely carried by voluntary lay organizations. Hinduism has generated similar organizations since the reform movements of the nineteenth century. The largest Muslim organizations in the world, Nadhatul-Ulama and Muhammadiyah in Indonesia, are also voluntary lay movements, and there are similar organizations in other Islamic countries.

Pluralism and the "Voluntary Imperative"

I have mentioned the "heretical imperative." Perhaps we could use another concept—the "voluntary imperative." It imposes itself wherever religious pluralism comes to predominate. Catholic observers have coined the term *Protestantization* to refer, usually pejoratively, to recent changes in their church. Stripped of its pejorative undertone, it is rather an apt term. Sometimes it describes doctrinal changes, most of which need not concern us here. But the term is most apt in describing social changes within the church—to wit, the role of an increasingly assertive laity, the transformation of the church into a de facto denomination, and one doctrinal change that is definitely relevant here—the theological undergirding of the norm of religious liberty. It is notable that the two individuals who were most influential in the affirmation of this norm by the Second Vatican Council came from the two homelands of modern democracy—Jacques Maritain from France and John Courtney Murray from the United States.

Americans in particular are prone to view the aforementioned developments as inexorable and irreversible—modernity generates pluralism, which generates the voluntary association, which then functions as a school for democracy. Eventually something like the New England town meeting will become a universal social and political norm. Alas, the empirical reality is more complicated. There are indeed pressures toward such a sociological trajectory. But the outcome of these pressures is not a foregone conclusion. There are possibilities of resistance, and under the right circumstances the pressures can be defeated and the trajectory reversed.

Resistances to pluralism have been conventionally subsumed under the category of "fundamentalism." I am uneasy about this term; it comes from a particular episode in the history of American Protestantism and is awkward when applied to other religious traditions (such as Islam). I will use it, because it has attained such wide currency, but I will define it more sharply: fundamentalism is any project to restore taken-for-grantedness in the individual's consciousness and therefore, necessarily, in his or her social and/or political environment. Such a project can have both religious and secular forms; the former concerns us here.

Religious fundamentalism can be more or less ambitious. In its more ambitious form it seeks to reshape the entire society in its image In recent history the last (so far) Christian version of this was the ideal of the Nationalists in the Spanish civil war—the ideal of a Catholic *reconquista* of Spain from the supposedly anti-Christian secularism of the republic. It was the last flowering of the "counter-Reformation baroque." It collapsed with the Franco regime, which intended to realize it, and today it is inconceivable that the Roman Catholic Church would again give its blessing to any comparable project. Nor are there other Christian analogues. (The notion, current in progressive circles today, that the Christian right in America has such intentions has little basis in the facts. No politically significant group in American evangelicalism intends to set up a theocratic regime, and fundamentalism as I define it has its adherents both on the left and on the right of the political spectrum in the United States.) But fundamentalist projects abound in the non-Western world.

There are sizable groupings in Russia who would like to set up a regime in which, once again, there would be a unity between church and state (a radical version of what in Orthodox political thought has been called *sinfonia*). Influential groups in Israel would reshape that society, with its entire political structure based on religious law, as a halachic state. Even more influential groups in India would replace its secular constitution with Hindutva, understood as a coercive Hinduism imposed on all citizens, including the large Muslim minority. And most importantly today, Islamist ideology seeks a theocratic state based on Islamic law, a *sharia* state imposed on the entire society. In its most ambitious version, this is the jihadist dream of a renewed caliphate embracing the entire Muslim world (and conceivably also lands that were once Muslim, notably the Balkans and "Al Andalus").

The chances for success of such projects vary from country to country. But it is possible to formulate one necessary condition for a successful realization: to convert an entire society into a support structure (what I would call a "plausibility structure") for a renewed taken-for-granted consensus, it will be necessary to establish a totalitarian regime. That is, the theocratic state will have to fully control all institutions in the society and, crucially, all channels of interaction and communication with the outside world. Under modern conditions this is very difficult, unless one wants to pay the price of catastrophic economic stagnation. The developments in Iran since the establishment of the Islamist regime clearly demonstrate the difficulty. It would be mistaken, though, to conclude that any project of religious totalitarianism is impossible. A regime willing to use ruthless and continuous repression, and indifferent to the material misery of its subjects, could yet pull such a project off.

The less ambitious form of religious fundamentalism is the sectarian one. It seeks to restore taken-for-grantedness in a subculture under its control, while the rest of society is, as it were, abandoned to the enemy. It is within the subculture that the individual can find the social consensus needed for cognitive and normative certainty. This, of course, has always been characteristic of sects. But in a society marked by pluralism the controls over interaction and communication with the outside have to be very rigorous indeed. The slightest relaxation of these controls can breach the protective dam against the pluralistic infection, alternative definitions of reality will then flood in, and the precariously maintained taken-for-grantedness can collapse overnight. Therefore, the denizens of the subculture must limit contacts with outsiders to a minimum, avoid all unnecessary conversation, and equally avoid all media of communication originating in the pluralistic world outside. In other words, what must be established and maintained is a kind of minitotalitarianism.

The sectarian project is thus not without its own serious difficulties, but these are less onerous than those confronting a project of *reconquista*. There are a good number of successful cases, in different religious traditions. Ideally for success, the fundamentalist group must have a territory, however small, under its control. This can be an isolated community (such as the Davidic compound in Waco, Texas), a circumscribed urban community (such as the ultra-Orthodox communities in Brooklyn or Mea Shearim in Jerusalem), a monastic or quasimonastic center (there are, of course, many of these in the Christian orbit), or an even larger geographical base (such as areas of northern Nigeria under Islamist control). But sectarian subcultures can also function without a territorial location, as long as the controls over interaction and communication are rigorously maintained. There are numerous examples of this in every major religious tradition—from Opus Dei to Sokka Gakkai, from the Lubavitcher Chabad to the Muslim Brotherhood (I cite these as sociological cases in point, without necessarily suggesting that they are morally equivalent).

Both society-wide totalitarianism and sectarian minitotalitarianism constitute difficult projects under modern conditions. The second is a better bet in terms of possible success. *Reconquista* totalitarianism is incompatible with pluralism, indeed must be implacably hostile to it. Minitotalitarianism is compatible with pluralism, but only to the extent that it accepts the pluralistic dominance in the larger society as long as its own subsociety is kept intact.

What follows from the argument of this essay is that the relation between pluralism (be it old or new) to democracy is complex. One cannot simply say that pluralism is either good or bad for democracy. It will be either, depending on the response to it by both religious and political institutions. As far as the latter is concerned, the distinction between liberal and illiberal democracy is very important here. A democratically elected regime can be intolerant of religious minorities (such as the difficulties of evangelical Protestants in Russia, in the Muslim world, and in India). Conversely, there have been tolerant authoritarian regimes (such as Prussia under Frederick the Great, Austria under Joseph II, and the Ottoman Empire on its better days).

Looking at any particular case, one must ask two key questions: how have the relevant religious traditions responded to the pluralistic challenge? I have argued here that acceptance (openly or de facto) of the voluntary principle will be decisive in this matter. One must then ask: what political interests have an affinity to this or that response, and what is the power of these interests to influence the course of events? For both historical and ideational reasons, Protestantism has had a comparative advantage in a positive adaptation to pluralism. This advantage continues today, notably in the global expansion of Pentecostalism and other versions of popular Protestantism. But there is also Protestantization in other religious traditions, even in that old adversary of Protestantism, the Roman Catholic Church. Thus both Protestant and non-Protestant religious institutions can, today, serve to bring about and solidify democracy. The most direct threat to democracy obviously comes from movements and regimes with an interest in establishing a totalitarian unity based on a reconquest *(reconquista)* of society in the name of this or that religious ideology. It would be a mistake to understand this threat exclusively in terms of radical Islam.

Notes

1. On globalization, see Peter L Berger and Samuel P. Huntington (eds), Many Globalizations: Cultural Diversity in the Contemporary World (Oxford: Oxford University Press, 2002a). On religious pluralism in the American context, see Robert Wuthnow, America and the Challenges of Religious Diversity (Princeton: Princeton University Press, 2005); and Diana L. Eck, A New Religious America: How a "Christian Country" Has Become the World's Most Religiously Diverse Nation (New York: Harper, 2001).

2. David Martin, Pentecostalism: The World Their Parish (Oxford: Blackwell, 2001). See also Harvey Cox, Fire from Heaven: The Rise of Pentecostal Spirituality and the Reshaping of Religion in the 21st Century (Cambridge, MA: Da Capo, 2001).

3.   Peter L. Berger, ed., The Desecularization of the World: Resurgent Religion and World Politics (Washington, DC: Ethics and Public Policy Center/ Grand Rapids: Eerdmans, 1999).
4.   See, for example, Rodney Stark, One True God: Historical Consequences of Monotheism (Princeton: Princeton University Press, 2003).
5.   "Baptists' Ardor for Evangelism Angers Some Jews and Hindus," New York Times, Dec. 4, 1999, Aso.
6.   Peter L. Berger, The Heretical Imperative: Contemporary Possibilities of Religious Affirmation (New York: Anchor, 1979).
7.   David Martin, "Integration and Fragmentierung: Religionsmuster in Europa," Transit 26 (Winter 2003–2004): 120–43.
8.   H. Neil McFarlane, Rush Hour of the Gods (New York: Macmillan, 1967).

Bibliography

Berger, Peter L., ed., *The Desecularization of the World: Resurgent Religion and World Politics.* Washington, DC: Ethics and Public Policy Center/Grand Rapids: Ferdmans, 1999.

———. *The Heretical Imperative: Contemporary Possibilities of Religious Affirmation.* New York: Anchor, 1980.

Berger, Peter L., and Samuel P. Huntington, eds. *Many Globalizations: Cultural Diversity in the Contemporary World.* Oxford: Oxford University Press, 2003.

Cox, Harvey. *Fire from Heaven: The Rise of Pentecostal Spirituality and the Reshaping of Religion in the 21st Century.* Cambridge, MA: Da Capo, 2001.

Eck, Diana L. *A New Religious America: How a "Christian Country" Has Become the World's Most Religiously Diverse Nation.* New York: Harper, 2001.

Martin, David. *Pentecostalism: The World Their Parish.* Oxford: Blackwell, 2001.

McFarlane, H. Neil. *Rush Hour of the Gods.* New York: Macmillan, 1967.

Stark, Rodney. *One True God: Historical Consequences of Monotheism.* Princeton: Princeton University Press, 2003.

Wuthnow, Robert. *America and the Challenges of Religious Diversity.* Princeton: Princeton University Press, 2005.

3

Religion and Desecularization

Because religion is so central to Peter L. Berger's works, he is often perceived solely as a sociologist of religion. However, it should be clear from the previous chapters that this perception is extremely one-sided. Indeed, on closer inspection, it turns out to be well-nigh false. As a sociologist, Berger deals with religion; as a lay theologian he deals with current problems of the churches; and as a confessed Christian he asks himself whether modern man can still believe. Within the framework of his research at the Protestant Academy in Bad Boll, Germany, in the 1950s, and after his return to the United States in 1956, Berger (1954b, 1962a, 1962b, 1963b, 1998b) engaged in the sociology of religion in that he analyzed trends in religiosity and in the membership of religious groups. Depending on the research question, these issues have also been addressed within the framework of research projects conducted under the auspices of the Institute on Culture, Religion and World Affairs (CURA) and its predecessors (see Chapter 4 below). In this context, religion is primarily regarded as an aspect of culture. *Empirically*, it is assigned to the broad category of values and convictions. However, Berger's *theoretical* approach to religion is characterized by a sociology-of-knowledge perspective. This is logical insofar as Berger and Kellner (1981: 84) point out that the sociology of religion "is actually a subsection of the sociology of knowledge."

3.1 Religion as a Human Product

Berger stresses that *The Sacred Canopy* (1967)—which was published in the same year as Thomas Luckmann's *Invisible Religion*—was not intended as a treatise on the sociology of religion, but rather as an attempt to "push to the final sociological consequence an understanding of religion as a historical product" (Berger 1967: vi). In other words, he perceives religion as the product of human activity, or, echoing

Feuerbach, as a "projection of human meanings" (ibid., 100). This social construction acquires its veneer of objective reality through processes of institutionalization and legitimation. Plausibility structures—that is, social relationships with significant and generalized others that serve to stabilize and support reality—are of fundamental importance in this regard, because the religious reality in question is supported and reinforced in communicative exchange with others.[1]

When applying to religion the theory of society derived from the sociology of knowledge, Berger focuses first on the process of nomization—that is, the establishment of a meaningful order—which he deems to be "the most important function of society" (1967: 22). He employs the term nomos as an antonym for Durkheim's anomie concept. Even though he did not introduce nomos until *The Sacred Canopy* (1967), it followed directly from the concept of the "integration of meaning" elaborated in *The Social Construction of Reality* (Berger & Luckmann 1966a). According to the authors of the latter work, the highest level of the integration of meaning is constituted by symbolic universes. These are characterized by the fact that they integrate into a "symbolic totality" the various provinces of meaning—including all experiences in "marginal situations not included in the everyday existence in society"—and all elements of the institutional order (ibid., 95–96).

Like Thomas Luckmann, Berger views religiosity in terms of the experience of transcendence. In so doing, he employs Schutz's notion of multiple realities, noting that "The reality of everyday life, therefore, is continuously surrounded by a penumbra of vastly different realities" (Berger 1967: 42). Although he shares Luckmann's view that man's capacity and yearning for symbolic self-transcendence is an anthropological prerequisite of religion, Berger criticizes the fact that Luckmann equates religion with symbolic self-transcendence, and questions the utility of such a broad definition (ibid., 176–77).[2] As an explicit alternative to Luckmann's perspective, Berger defines religion as "the human enterprise by which a sacred cosmos is established" (ibid., 25).

Elevated to the status of the taken for granted, nomization tends toward cosmization—that is, "the merging of socially established meanings with fundamental meanings inherent in the universe" (loc. cit.). All nomizations—and, even more so, all cosmizations—serve the purpose of protecting the arduously established order from chaos, and of making sure that it does not descend (once again) into the abyss of anomie and meaninglessness (ibid., 26–27). As a human construction, this protective order is inherently precarious. It is permanently threatened by marginal situations that can be caused by external circumstances or can arise from states of consciousness that can be experienced only subjectively. As Berger (1967: 25) argues following Mircea Eliade (1957) and, in particular, Rudolf Otto (1963), the endowment of cosmization with a sacred quality implies the postulation of "a mysterious and awesome power other than man yet related to him, which is believed to reside in certain objects of experience." Secular symbolic meaning systems, such as philosophy or science, also construct a canopy of meaning. However, what distinguishes religion from secular symbolic universes of meaning is the fact that it provides a divine cosmos, a "*sacred* canopy." Berger traces the fine and gradual differentiation between the sacred and the supernatural, attempting to grasp the former as "otherness," as something "radically transcendent, not to be identified with any natural or human phenomena" (1967: 87, 115–16; cf. also 1974c). Because he declares the sacred to be the substance of religion, Berger (1967: 177) labels his definition of religion *substantive* in contrast to Thomas Luckmann's anthropologically—rather than institutionally—grounded *functional* definition. What makes Berger's definition sociologically cumbersome is the fact that there is a sociologically inaccessible aspect inherent in it. In *The Heretical Imperative* he argues that:

> *Religion can be understood as a human projection because it is communicated in human symbols. But this very communication is motivated by an experience in which a metahuman reality is injected into human life.* (1979: 48; emphasis in the original)

In his analysis of the reified nature of religion, on the other hand, Berger finds himself on sociologically fortified terrain. In his view, the fact that religion has been "one of the most effective bulwarks against anomie" is directly related to its "alienating propensity" (1967: 87). Moreover, religious legitimations are particularly predestined to mystify—that is to transform into transcendent facticities—originally human products such as institutions and institutionalized roles. In *The Social Construction of Reality* (1966a), Berger and Luckmann drew a clear line between objectivation as an anthropological constant, and alienation in the sense of estrangement.[3] Later, in *The Sacred Canopy* (1967: 85), Berger distinguishes "two ways in which estrangement may proceed":

> . . . one in which the strangeness of world and self can be reappropriated (*zurueckgeholt*) by the "recollection" that both world and

self are products of one's own activity—the other in which such reappropriation is no longer possible, and in which the social world and socialized self confront the individual as inexorable facticities analogous to the facticities of nature. The latter process may be called alienation.

Berger stresses that religion cannot be automatically equated with alienation. However, following Rudolf Otto (1963), he argues that, precisely because the sacred can be experienced as overwhelming otherness, religious projections have an inherent tendency to confront human life with something completely alien, thereby also alienating man from himself. Hence, it is the sociology-of-knowledge derivation of religion from processes of nomization, cosmization, and sacralization that places religion close to alienation, and Berger's position close to that of Feuerbach and Marx. This caused him some unease, because alienation was very much en vogue when *The Sacred Canopy* (1967) was published. The unease was due to the fact Berger sharply rejects central Marxist positions—for example, the perception of religion as a means of satisfying needs—a thesis also supported by behaviorist theories. In Berger's view, religion is not merely a cozy abode. Nor can his understanding of religion be summed up by saying that his actual point of aim is to expose psychological explanations of religious experiences as an attempt—which enjoys particular success in the age of modernity—to establish a hegemonic system of interpretation. For him, religion is more: It has a substance that can be described as a holy awe.

3.2 An Anthropological Theology

Berger's argument in *The Precarious Vision* (1961b) that religion must be differentiated from (Christian) faith was strongly influenced by the neo-orthodox Protestant theologian Karl Barth.[4] In *The Sacred Canopy* (1967: 183–84), Berger explicitly distances himself from this postulate, acknowledging that "in any empirical discipline the 'Christian faith' is simply another case of the phenomenon 'religion.' Empirically, the differentiation makes no sense." Concerned that *The Sacred Canopy* might be misconstrued as "a treatise on atheism" (1969a: ix–x), Berger added a second appendix, in which he adopts a position oriented toward the liberal early-nineteenth-century Protestant theologian Friedrich Schleiermacher. He contends that theology cannot ignore the sociological insight that religion is a human projection whose objective reality is grounded in specific infrastructures and whose subjective reality is maintained by specific plausibility structures (1967: 184).

From this it follows that, unless they want to have to take refuge in orthodoxies, theologians have no alternative but to expose themselves to the "vertigo of relativity," which was triggered by historical scholarship and intensified by sociologists (ibid., 182).

As Berger makes clear in *The Heretical Imperative* (1979: 56ff.), he considers the secularizing theologian's flight into a "reductive faith"— that is, into the relativization, or even the abandonment, of the truth claim—to be just as unacceptable as the neo-orthodox flight into a "deductive faith" that *re*affirms the objective authority of a religious tradition by restoring it to the status of an a priori. In the modern context, he regards the deductive option as backward looking in the literal sense of the word. In his view, theologians who take this route maneuver themselves into an untenable position because the memory of the interval when tradition was relativized and weakened cannot be erased (ibid., 73–74). As he points out in *The Sacred Canopy* (1967: 184):

> The theologian is consequently deprived of the psychologically liberating possibility of either radical commitment or radical negation. What he is left with, I think, is the necessity for a step-by-step re-evaluation of the traditional affirmations in terms of his own cognitive criteria (which need not necessarily be those of a putative "modern consciousness").

Berger (1979: 58) is adamant that there is only one theological method "that promises both to face and to overcome the challenges of the modern situation," namely the "inductive option." In *A Rumor of Angels* (1969a), he sketches a preliminary outline of this concept, which has an anthropological starting point and proceeds inductively from everyday human experiences. He calls these experiences "signals of transcendence"—that is, "phenomena that are to be found within the domain of our 'natural' reality but that appear to point beyond that reality" (ibid., 53). Berger (ibid., 54–72) recognizes such signals in the gesture of a mother reassuring her child that "everything is in order"; in the world of joyful play, which "appears to suspend, or bracket, the reality of our 'living towards death'"; in hope against all hope; in humor; and in the certainty that damnation, in the sense of divine punishment, awaits the perpetrators of inhumane acts. This mundane list reveals that Berger does not conceive of "signals of transcendence" as mystical, miraculous experiences, but rather—in accordance with his sociology-of-knowledge perspective—as the experiences of everyday people living everyday lives.

From a sociological perspective, Berger's use of the term inductive is misleading because it seems to imply that the existence of what he calls "an other reality" can be inferred from human experiences. Replying to criticism along these lines voiced by Gaede (1986), Berger (1986d: 232) stresses that "inductive" merely denotes a procedure whereby one takes ordinary human experiences as a starting point and searches in them for "signals of transcendence." However, it is not too outlandish to assume that, when he chose the term, the association with inductive reasoning was intended. As he explained in *A Rumor of Angels* (1969a: 57), "Put simply: Inductive faith moves from human experience to statements about God, deductive faith from statements about God to interpretations of human experience."[5]

In that book (ibid., 47), Berger stresses that the inductive approach to religious thought by no means constitutes empirical theology, but rather "theology with a very high empirical sensitivity that seeks to correlate its propositions with what can be empirically known." Ten years later, in *The Heretical Imperative* (1979), he elaborates in great detail on the three theological strategies—deduction, reduction, and induction—adumbrated in *A Rumor of Angels* (1969a). He illustrates these "options for religious thought in the pluralistic situation" (1979: 56) by means of paradigmatic examples from Protestant theology. The ongoing conversation with his previous writings that he conducts in *The Heretical Imperative* is typical of the way Berger works. *A Rumor of Angels* (1969a) was also motivated by a desire to pick up a trail that he had laid in a previous book—*A Sacred Canopy* (1967)—where he attempted to "break through the assumptions of modern secularism from within" (1979: x).

In *A Sacred Canopy* (1967: 180), Berger stresses that "sociological theory must, by its own logic, view religion as a human projection." He argues that sociologists must strictly bracket "the possibility that the projected meanings may refer to something other than the being of its projector," because it is beyond the reach of a strictly empirical discipline. He describes this approach as "methodological atheism," a term derived from Anton Zijderveld. Obviously anxious that the qualifier *methodological* might be overlooked, he emphatically states that "to say that religion is a human project does not logically preclude the possibility that the projected meanings may have an ultimate status independent of man (loc. cit.)." Berger elaborates this point in *A Rumor of Angels* (1969a: 46), arguing that:

It is logically possible . . . that both perspectives may coexist, each within its particular frame of reference. What appears as a human projection in one may appear as a reflection of divine realities in another. The logic of the first perspective does not preclude the possibility of the latter.

Applying a sociology-of-knowledge perspective to theology, Berger (ibid., 40) deems it untenable, to relativize religious tradition by assigning it to antiquated consciousness, as radical or secular theologians have done. He argues that the type of modern consciousness that has problems with the supernatural, is, itself, a time-bound phenomenon, in other words an expression of the *zeitgeist*, and he notes that:

> One (perhaps literally) redeeming feature of sociological perspective is that relativizing analysis, in being pushed to its final consequence, bends back upon itself. The relativizers are relativized, the debunkers are debunked—indeed, relativization itself is somehow liquidated. What follows is *not*, as some of the early sociologists of knowledge feared, a total paralysis of thought. Rather, it is a new freedom and flexibility in asking questions of truth. (ibid., 42)

Hence Berger's conclusion that the sociology of knowledge actually "offers a measure of liberation from the taken-for-granted certitudes of our time" (ibid., 45).

3.3 The Possibility of Faith

Even though Berger renounced a long time ago the neo-orthodox position that he adopted in *The Precarious Vision* (1961b), one question raised in that book—"Can a truly contemporary person be a Christian?"—is still on his agenda. Expressed in broader terms, the question that Berger asks himself is how true faith is possible under conditions of pluralism and, therefore, in an "age of credulity" (the subtitle of his book *A Far Glory* (1992b) was *The Quest for Faith in an Age of Credulity).* He formulated a general answer to this question in *The Heretical Imperative* (1979) and elaborated on it further in *A Far Glory* (1992b: 104):

> Modernity, like every historical moment, is very mixed, and includes specific elements that I, for one, would describe as retrogressive. But it happens to be the situation in which we find ourselves. We should not deny it, or delude ourselves that we are something else. To accept this situation means accepting what I have elsewhere referred to as

"the heretical imperative," namely the fact that it forces us to make choices. But to say that we ought simply to accept the modern situation is too pejorative. Not everything about this situation deserves to be deplored. And above all, as I have tried to argue, the modern situation has brought us an unprecedented freedom.

Berger expresses his personal response to this challenge with the help of Luther's doctrine of salvation "by faith alone" (*sola fide*). For him, the alternative to the quest for certainty in "an infallible church, an inerrant scripture, or an irresistible personal experience" (2004a: vii) is to live with uncertainty in faith, because "Therein lies the secret of a distinctively Protestant freedom" (1998b: 33; our translation; cf. also 2004a: 141). Among all the available alternatives, he opts personally for a faith that comes closest to this Lutheran variant of Protestantism without being completely identical to it. In the preface to *Questions of Faith. A Skeptical Affirmation of Christianity* (2004a: viii), he openly admits to being a heterodox Protestant:

> I feel uncomfortable with all available theological labels and ecclesial affiliations. My biographical roots are in Lutheranism, and I would still identify myself as Lutheran, albeit with great reservation. . . . I most feel at home in the tradition of Friedrich Schleiermacher, because this tradition embodies precisely the balance between skepticism and affirmation that, for me, defines the only acceptable way of being Christian without emigrating from modernity.

In this book, which is organized around phrases from the Apostles' Creed, Berger explains the theological reasons for his "choice of location on the theological map."

Ultimately, Berger's main focus is on the experience of an other reality, a reality that by virtue of its benevolence makes marginal situations—first and foremost, death—bearable. As different as religions might be, almost all of them give the *faithful* the prospect that life will not end in nothing and that death marks the transition to an other, less distressing, more fulfilled, happier reality. According to Berger, this also applies to nirvana in Hinduism. Religious virtuosis (Max Weber's term) tell of encounters with God, an angel, or other supernatural beings. They often feel that these encounters were inflicted upon them, and they experience them as frightening—which makes the experiences all the more real. The average human being, by contrast, can never be sure of coming into contact with this other reality. Hence, for most ordinary people faith means not knowing.

Analytically, Berger does not tend to draw a clear line between religious experience and other, for example, spiritual, experiences. In his view, when people describe themselves as spiritual rather than religious, it is mainly an indication of their dissatisfaction with their church and sometimes also an expression of their quest for a harmonious, balanced life (2004a: 122–23). However, provided their spiritual orientation addresses aspects of the supernatural and the sacred, it can, in fact, be classified as religious—even if it is directed toward esoteric doctrines, which are often characterized by a certain degree of eclecticism. Berger (1986d: 231) conceives of the supernatural and the sacred as intersecting circles, arguing that "Only the common area contains what has been known as religious experiences." He labels as parapsychology those orientations, such as magic, that focus exclusively on the supernatural "without the sense of the sacred." And he points out that secularization leads to the "sanctification of such secular entities as science, or the nation, or the revolutionary movement" without the aspect of the supernatural (loc. cit.).

Hammond (1986) criticizes Berger's definition of religion, arguing that it recognizes as religion only those encounters with the sacred in which—metaphorically speaking—the holy awe stems from the supernatural (and not, for example, from the experience of a mass event). This criticism is probably due to the fact that Berger merely implies his phenomenological starting point rather than making it explicit. Following Schutz's notion of "multiple realities" (Schutz & Natanson 1982), Berger regards the supernatural reality postulated by religion as one of the great transcendencies that cross the boundaries of the everyday life-world. The everyday life-world represents the "paramount reality" in which people spend most of their time. As wide-awake adults in everyday life we find ourselves in "the relatively natural attitude" and are surrounded by our fellow-men. The everyday life-world is the world in which we work and of which we can dispose. In *A Rumor of Angels* (1969a: 42), Berger devotes a lot of space to explaining why contemporary consciousness is incapable of conceiving of either angels or demons. However, he neglects to describe phenomenologically the type of consciousness that is capable of doing so.

3.4 Desecularization

Until the 1970s, Berger—like most sociologists of religion—supported the thesis that modernity necessarily leads to secularization. He considered that the presumed secularizing effect of modernity was rendered plausible by Max Weber's thesis of the "disenchantment of the world." In *The Sacred Canopy* (1967: 111), Berger agrees that Protestantism, which had divested itself of "the three most ancient and powerful concomitants of the sacred—mystery, miracle, and magic," was a major driving force behind the disenchantment of the Western world. However, he points out that the roots of the process can be traced back to the Old Testament (ibid., 113).

Berger (ibid., 197) defines secularization as "a process by which sectors of society and culture are removed from the domination of religious institutions and symbols." On the one hand, therefore, secularization is a process of religious de-institutionalization. By pointing out that this process affects the levels of culture and symbols, Berger makes it clear that sociocultural secularization also manifests itself on the level of individual consciousness. Hence "the modern West has produced an increasing number of individuals who look upon the world and their own lives without the benefit of religious interpretations" (ibid., 108).[6]

In his distinction between inner and outer secularization, Berger follows Luckmann (1969),[7] who debunked secularization as a modern myth much earlier than Berger did. Luckmann's consistently skeptical attitude toward the secularization paradigm is another major difference between his sociology of religion and Berger's. While both men have always agreed that the link between modernity and pluralism is indisputable because modernization functions intrinsically as a carrier of pluralism, it was not until the early 1970s that Berger radically changed his thinking on secularization (1971a, 1971b). His revised stance was that pluralism correlated historically with secularization only in Western Europe, and that secularization theory had been developed mainly by European intellectuals, who had made the fundamental mistake of elevating this historical exception to the status of a rule, thereby extrapolating from Western Europe to the rest of the world.

In *Religious America, Secular Europe? A Theme and Variations* (Berger, Davie & Fokas 2008b), which summarized the findings of a CURA project on Eurosecularity, Berger and his coauthors, Grace Davie and Effie Fokas, analyze the differences between the exceptional case—Europe—and the United States. In a chapter that he contributed to the book (2008b: 9–10), Berger argues that, like any other important historical phenomenon, secularization cannot be explained mono-causally. He identifies a comprehensive set of factors that led to the Western and Central Europe becoming a geographic exceptional case.

Following Alexis de Tocqueville, Berger considers the relationship between church and state to be a particularly important causal factor. He points out that, even in colonial America, no church has ever succeeded in achieving a dominant position that would have enabled it to develop an exclusive relationship with the temporal power. The Puritans' attempt to establish Calvinism as the state church in Massachusetts failed, as did a similar attempt on the part of the Anglicans in Virginia. This failure was due not to the postulate of tolerance but rather to the opposition of competing religions. The First Amendment to the American Constitution ideologically legitimated freedom of religion and the separation of church and state. As a consequence, the churches became "voluntary associations." Herein lies a fundamental difference between the United States and Europe. Because established churches existed in most countries in Protestant and Catholic Europe into the twentieth century—and indeed still exist in England, Denmark, Norway, and Finland, for example—the church was closely identified with authority. Berger (ibid., 16) argues that this is an important element of the explanation of Eurosecularity, because "where religion is closely identified with the state, resentments against the latter almost inevitably come to include the former."

Besides a number of other causal factors, Berger repeatedly stresses the role of intellectuals. In his aforementioned contribution to *Religious America, Secular Europe?* (Berger et al. 2008b: 17–18), he notes that the French Enlightenment was sharply anti-clerical and that the intelligentsia in Europe had been a secularizing force. The secularizing attitude of European intellectuals had spread to their counterparts in the United States: "One may say then that the American intelligentsia has been 'Europeanized' in its attitude to religion as in other matters." However, he points out that, compared to the intelligentsia in Europe, American intellectuals are much less influential.

As a result of the expansion of education, the secularizing attitude of the intelligentsia spreads to other social strata because the plausibility of religious experiences is weakened when cognitive elites have a secularized worldview (cf. Wuthnow et al. 1984: 64). However, the secularized international intellectual elite, which can be conceived of as a "world intellectual culture" (Berger & Huntington 2002a: 50), represents the exceptional case in the secularization context.

According to Berger, this empirically well-supported finding is the main reason why so many sociologists of religion continued to adhere to secularization theory despite numerous empirically grounded counter-arguments. In view of the explosive spread of religions—especially Islam and Pentecostalism—he not only considers that secularization theory has been shown to be false (or, as he would put it, "blown out of the water"). In *The Desecularization of the World: Resurgent Religion and World Politics* (1999) he also explicitly postulates the existence of a counter-trend, namely desecularization or counter-secularization. And in a paper entitled "Reflections on Sociology of Religion Today" (2001b), he declares the interplay between secularizing and counter-secularizing forces to be one of the most important questions for contemporary sociology of religion.

However, Berger by no means denies the immense consequences of modernization, not only for those religions that had a monopolistic position in premodern societies. As far back as 1963, in a paper entitled "A Market Model for the Analysis of Ecumenicity" (cf. 1963c), he first drew attention to the change in the relationship between church and state, between clergy and laity, and between the religious institutions themselves. These institutions find themselves in a competitive situation that obliges them to present their respective offerings of meaning in an attractive way. Under these conditions, lay people can either choose between different religious purveyors of meaning, or put together their own eclectic spiritual package. As a result, the religious institutions lose their power to impose sanctions. Moreover, their economic power diminishes due to declining membership.

Religions can respond to this competitive situation by opening up or closing themselves off. In Berger's view, neither isolation from the outside world nor exclusionary closure has a lasting prospect for success. The practical advice he gives to church institutions is to engage in ecumenical dialog with competitors without sacrificing the fundamental tenets of their respective religions. This presupposes prior differentiation between intrinsic and extrinsic elements of faith. What is deemed to be the ultimate truth must be defended; what is considered negotiable can be negotiated (cf. 1992b: 63).

On the level of individual consciousness, Berger considers the pluralization of life-worlds—which he first addressed in *The Homeless Mind* (1973a)—to be the gravest effect of modernity. Religions and religiosity are particularly affected because pluralism "undermines all taken-for-granted certainties" (cf. 2001b). Berger stresses that, while pluralism does not inexorably lead to secularization—that is, to "a decline in religion both in society and in the minds of individuals" (1999: 2)—it does, however, bring about a situation in which religious convictions can no longer be taken for granted, but must be chosen. In other words, they become a matter of preference: "I would propose that pluralism affects the 'how' rather than the 'what' of religious belief and practice—and that is something quite different from secularization" (2002b: 296).

Notes

1. The American sociologist of religion Robert Wuthnow draws attention to the fundamental importance of plausibility structures—and, thus, of the social element—for Berger's sociological theory of religion. Admittedly, Wuthnow (1986: 140) cautiously criticizes the fact that precisely this element of the theory could give rise to a suspicion of determinism. Moreover, he also points out that the subjective dimension of, and the rational-cognitive approach to, religion are overemphasized. (The rational-cognitive approach may stem from Berger's "Austrian Lutheranism.") Nonetheless, Wuthnow's critique of Berger's sociology is unrecognizably motivated by the intention to make his approach accessible to American sociology (of religion).

2. Because such a definition implies that "everything genuinely human is ipso facto religious and the only nonreligious phenomena in the human sphere are those that are grounded in man's animal nature, or more precisely, that part of his biological constitution that he has *in common* with other animals" (1967: 177). For an account of the way in which Berger's concept of religion differs from Luckmann's, and for critical stances in this definition dispute, cf. Schnettler (2006: 55–58) and Dobbelaere and Lauwers (1973).

3. For a thorough analysis of the conceptual implications of objectification, objectivation, alienation, and reification, see Berger and Pullberg (1965e).

4. In true Barthian fashion, the early, neo-orthodox, Berger declared: "What the proclamation of Jesus Christ demands is faith. The religious enterprise circumvents this demand and seeks to meet God on other grounds. In other words, religion is lack of faith" (1961b: 166). As the later, heterodox-liberal, Berger notes in *The Heretical Imperative* (1979: 77), Barth insisted that "*all* human religion is unbelief and Christian faith is not to be subsumed under the category of religion."

5. On the other hand, Berger (1986d: 232) concedes the justification of Gaede's (1981) criticism that his threefold typology comprising deductive, reductive, and inductive modes of theologizing was incomplete. Gaede had criticized that this typology conflated two heterogeneous themes—the deductive/inductive and the orthodox/heterodox. On reflection, Berger acknowledges that there are actually four options for religious thought under conditions of pluralism. He calls them deductive orthodox (formerly deductive); deductive heterodox (formerly reductive); inductive heterodox (formerly inductive), and—the new variant—inductive orthodox, whereby the last variant connotes movement from personal experience to an orthodox attitude.

6. Because the book was written before he realized that secularization theory was mistaken, Berger himself now considers the second part—devoted to secularization—to be radically outdated (cf. 2011: 100).

7. Berger also repeatedly concurs with Luckmann's thesis of the privatization of religion; cf. (1967: 208), Wuthnow et al. (1984: 61).

The Desecularization of the World: A Global Overview

by Peter L. Berger

A few years ago the first volume coming out of the so-called Funda-mentalism Project landed on my desk. The Fundamentalism Project was very generously funded by the MacArthur Foundation and chaired by Martin Marty, the distinguished church historian at the University of Chicago. A number of very reputable scholars took part in it, and the published results are of generally excellent quality. But my con-templation of this first volume gave me what has been called an "*aha!* experience." The book was very big, sitting there on my desk—a "book-weapon," the kind that could do serious injury. So I asked myself, why would the MacArthur Foundation shell out several million dollars to support an international study of religious fundamentalists?

Two answers came to mind. The first was obvious and not very interesting. The MacArthur Foundation is a very progressive outfit; it understands fundamentalists to be anti-progressive; the Project, then, was a matter of knowing one's enemies. But there was also a more interesting answer. "Fundamentalism" is considered a strange, hard-to-understand phenomenon; the purpose of the Project was to delve into this alien world and make it more understandable. But to whom? *Who* finds this world strange? Well, the answer to *that* question was easy: people to whom the officials of the MacArthur Foundation normally talk, such as professors at elite American universities. And with this came the aha! experience. The concern that must have led to this Project was based on an upside-down perception of the world, according to which "fundamentalism" (which, when all is said and done, usually refers to any sort of passionate religious movement) is a rare, hard-to-explain thing. But a look either at history or at the contemporary world reveals that what is rare is not the phenomenon

61

itself but knowledge of it. The difficult-to-understand phenomenon is not Iranian mullahs but American university professors—it might be worth a multi-million-dollar project to try to explain that!

Mistakes of Secularization Theory

My point is that the assumption that we live in a secularized world is false. The world today, with some exceptions to which I will come presently, is as furiously religious as it ever was, and in some places more so than ever. This means that a whole body of literature by historians and social scientists loosely labeled "secularization theory" is essentially mistaken. In my early work I contributed to this literature. I was in good company—most sociologists of religion had similar views, and we had good reasons for holding them. Some of the writings we produced still stand up. (As I like to tell my students, one advantage of being a social scientist, as against being, say, a philosopher or a theologian, is that you can have as much fun when your theories are falsified as when they are verified!)

Although the term "secularization theory" refers to works from the 1950s and 1960s, the key idea of the theory can indeed be traced to the Enlightenment. That idea is simple: Modernization necessarily leads to a decline of religion, both in society and in the minds of individuals. And it is precisely this key idea that has turned out to be wrong. To be sure, modernization has had some secularizing effects, more in some places than in others. But it has also provoked powerful movements of counter-secularization. Also, secularization on the societal level is not necessarily linked to secularization on the level of individual consciousness. Certain religious institutions have lost power and influence in many societies, but both old and new religious beliefs and practices have nevertheless continued in the lives of individuals, sometimes taking new institutional forms and sometimes leading to great explosions of religious fervor. Conversely, religiously identified institutions can play social or political roles even when very few people believe or practice the religion that the institutions represent. To say the least, the relation between religion and modernity is rather complicated.

The proposition that modernity necessarily leads to a decline of religion is, in principle, "value free." That is, it can be affirmed both by people who think it is good news and by people who think it is very bad news. Most Enlightenment thinkers and most progressive-minded people ever since have tended toward the idea that secularization is a good thing, at least insofar as it does away with religious phenomena that are "backward," "superstitious," or "reactionary" (a religious residue purged of these negative characteristics may still be deemed acceptable). But religious people, including those with very traditional or orthodox beliefs, have also affirmed the modernity/secularity linkage, and have greatly bemoaned it. Some have then defined modernity as the enemy, to be fought whenever possible. Others have, on the contrary, seen modernity as some kind of invincible world-view to which religious beliefs and practices should adapt themselves. In other words, *rejection* and *adaptation* are two strategies open to religious communities in a world understood to be secularized. As is always the case when strategies are based on mistaken perceptions of the terrain, both strategies have had very doubtful results.

It is possible, of course, to reject any number of modern ideas and values theoretically, but making this rejection stick in the lives of people is much harder. To do that requires one of two strategies. The first is *religious revolution:* one tries to take over society as a whole and make one's counter-modern religion obligatory for everyone—a difficult enterprise in most countries in the contemporary world. (Franco tried in Spain and failed; the mullahs are still at it in Iran and a couple of other places.) And this *does* have to do with modernization, which brings about very heterogeneous societies and a quantum leap in intercultural communication, two factors favoring pluralism and *not* favoring the establishment (or reestablishment) of religious monopolies. The other possible way of getting people to reject modern ideas and values in their lives is to create *religious subcultures* designed to keep out the influences of the outside society. That is a somewhat more promising exercise than religious revolution, but it too is fraught with difficulty. Modern culture is a very powerful force, and an immense effort is required to maintain enclaves with an airtight defense system. Ask the Amish in eastern Pennsylvania. Or ask a Hasidic rabbi in the Williamsburg section of Brooklyn.

Interestingly, secularization theory has also been falsified by the results of adaptation strategies by religious institutions. If we really lived in a highly secularized world, then religious institutions could be expected to survive to the degree that they manage to adapt to secularity. That has been the empirical assumption of adaptation strategies. What has in fact occurred is that, by and large, religious communities have survived and even flourished to the degree that they have *not* tried to adapt themselves to the alleged requirements of a secularized world. To put it simply, experiments with secularized religion have generally

63

failed; religious movements with beliefs and practices dripping with reactionary supernaturalism (the kind utterly beyond the pale at self-respecting faculty parties) have widely succeeded.

The Catholic Church vs. Modernity

The struggle with modernity in the Roman Catholic Church nicely illustrates the difficulties of various strategies. In the wake of the Enlightenment and its multiple revolutions, the initial response by the Church was militant and then defiant rejection. Perhaps the most magnificent moment of that defiance came in 1870, when the First Vatican Council solemnly proclaimed the infallibility of the Pope and the immaculate conception of Mary, literally in the face of the Enlightenment about to occupy Rome in the shape of the army of Victor Emmanuel I. (The disdain was mutual. If you have ever visited the Roman monument to the Bersaglieri, the elite army units that occupied the Eternal City in the name of the Italian *Risorgimento,* you may have noticed the placement of the heroic figure in his Bersaglieri uniform—he is positioned so that his behind points exactly toward the Vatican.)

The Second Vatican Council, almost a hundred years later, considerably modified this rejectionist stance, guided as it was by the notion of *aggiornamento,* bringing the Church up to date—that is, up to date with the modern world. (I remember asking a Protestant theologian what he thought would happen at the Council—this was before it had convened; he replied that he didn't know but he was sure they would not read the minutes of the last meeting!) The Second Vatican Council was supposed to open windows, specifically the windows of the Catholic subculture that had been constructed when it became clear that the overall society could not be reconquered. In the United States, this Catholic subculture has been quite impressive right up to the very recent past. The trouble with opening windows is that you can't control what comes in, and a lot has come in—indeed, the whole turbulent world of modern culture—that has been very troubling to the Church. Under the current pontificate the Church has been steering a nuanced course between rejection and adaptation, with mixed results in different countries.

This is as good a point as any to mention that all my observations here are intended to be "value free"; that is, I am trying to look at the current religious scene objectively. For the duration of this exercise I have put aside my own religious beliefs. As a sociologist of religion,

I find it probable that Rome had to do some reining in on the level of both doctrine and practice, in the wake of the institutional disturbances that followed Vatican II. To say this, however, in no way implies my theological agreement with what has been happening in the Roman Catholic Church under the present pontificate. Indeed, if I were Roman Catholic, I would have considerable misgivings about these developments. But I am a liberal Protestant (the adjective refers to my religious position and not to my politics), and I have no immediate existential stake in what is happening within the Roman community. I am speaking here as a sociologist, in which capacity I can claim a certain competence; I have no theological credentials.

THE GLOBAL RELIGIOUS SCENE

On the international religious scene, it is conservative or orthodox or traditionalist movements that are on the rise almost everywhere. These movements are precisely the ones that rejected an *aggiornamento* with modernity as defined by progressive intellectuals. Conversely, religious movements and institutions that have made great efforts to conform to a perceived modernity are almost everywhere on the decline. In the United States this has been a much commented upon fact, exemplified by the decline of so-called mainline Protestantism and the concomitant rise of Evangelicalism; but the United States is by no means unusual in this.

Nor is Protestantism. The conservative thrust in the Roman Catholic Church under John Paul II has borne fruit in both number of converts and renewed enthusiasm among native Catholics, especially in non-Western countries. Following the collapse of the Soviet Union there occurred a remarkable revival of the Orthodox Church in Russia. The most rapidly growing Jewish groups, both in Israel and in the Diaspora, are Orthodox. There have been similarly vigorous upsurges of conservative religion in all the other major religious communities— Islam, Hinduism, Buddhism—as well as revival movements in smaller communities (such as Shinto in Japan and Sikhism in India). These developments differ greatly in their social and political implications. What they have in common is their unambiguously *religious* inspiration. Consequently, taken together they provide a massive falsification of the idea that modernization and secularization are cognate phenomena. At the very least they show that counter-secularization is at least as important a phenomenon in the contemporary world as secularization.

Both in the media and in scholarly publications, these movements are often subsumed under the category of "fundamentalism." This is not a felicitous term, not only because it carries a pejorative undertone but also because it derives from the history of American Protestantism, where it has a specific reference that is distortive if extended to other religious traditions. All the same, the term has some suggestive use if one wishes to explain the aforementioned developments. It suggests a combination of several features—great religious passion, a defiance of what others have defined as the *Zeitgeist,* and a return to traditional sources of religious authority. These are indeed common features across cultural boundaries. And they do reflect the presence of secularizing forces, since they must be understood as a reaction *against* those forces. (In that sense, at least, something of the old secularization theory may be said to hold up, in a rather back-handed way.) This interplay of secularizing and counter-secularizing forces is, I would contend, one of the most important topics for a sociology of contemporary religion, but far too large to consider here. I can only drop a hint: Modernity, for fully understandable reasons, undermines all the old certainties; uncertainty is a condition that many people find very hard to bear; therefore, any movement (not only a religious one) that promises to provide or to renew certainty has a ready market.

Differences Among Thriving Movements

While the aforementioned common features are important, an analysis of the social and political impact, of the various religious upsurges must also take full account of their differences. This becomes clear when one looks at what are arguably the two most dynamic religious upsurges in the world today, the Islamic and the Evangelical; the comparison also underlines the weakness of the category of "fundamentalism" as applied to both.

The Islamic upsurge, because of its more immediately obvious political ramifications, is better. known. Yet it would be a serious error to see it only through a political lens. It is an impressive revival of emphatically *religious* commitments. And it is of vast geographical scope, affecting every single Muslim country from North Africa to Southeast Asia. It continues to gain converts, especially in sub-Saharan Africa (where it is often in head-on competition with Christianity). It is becoming very visible in the burgeoning Muslim communities in Europe and, to a much lesser extent, in North America. Everywhere it is bringing about a restoration, not only of Islamic beliefs but of distinctively Islamic life-styles, which in many ways directly contradict modern ideas—such as ideas about the relation of religion and the state, the role of women, moral codes of everyday behavior, and the boundaries of religious and moral tolerance. The Islamic revival is by no means restricted to the less modernized or "backward" sectors of society, as progressive intellectuals still like to think. On the contrary, it is very strong in cities with a high degree of modernization, and in a number of countries it is particularly visible among people with Western-style higher education—in Egypt and Turkey, for example, many daughters of secularized professionals are putting on the veil and other accoutrements of Islamic modesty.

Yet there are also great differences within the movement. Even within the Middle East, the Islamic heartland, there are both religiously and politically important differences between Sunni and Shiite revivals—Islamic conservatism means very different things in, say, Saudi Arabia and Iran. Away from the Middle East, the differences become even greater. Thus in Indonesia, the most populous Muslim country in the world, a very powerful revival movement, the Nudhat'ul-Ulama, is avowedly pro-democracy and pro-pluralism, the very opposite of what is commonly viewed as Muslim "fundamentalism." Where the political circumstances allow this, there is in many places a lively discussion about the relation of Islam to various modern realities, and there are sharp disagreements among individuals who are equally committed to a revitalized Islam. Still, for reasons deeply grounded in the core of the tradition, it is probably fair to say that, on the whole, Islam has had a difficult time coming to terms with key modern institutions, such as pluralism, democracy, and the market economy.

The Evangelical upsurge is just as breathtaking in scope. Geographically that scope is even wider. It has gained huge numbers of converts in East Asia—in all the Chinese communities (including, despite severe persecution, mainland China) and in South Korea, the Philippines, across the South Pacific, throughout sub-Saharan Africa (where it is often synthetized with elements of traditional African religion), apparently in parts of ex-Communist Europe. But the most remarkable success has occurred in Latin America; there are now thought to be between forty and fifty million Evangelical Protestants south of the U.S. border, the great majority of them first-generation Protestants. The most numerous component within the Evangelical upsurge is Pentecostalism, which combines biblical orthodoxy and a rigorous morality with an ecstatic form of worship and an emphasis on spiritual healing.

Especially in Latin America, conversion to Protestantism brings about a cultural transformation—new attitudes toward work and consumption, a new educational ethos, and a violent rejection of traditional *machismo* (women play a key role in the Evangelical churches).

The origins of this worldwide Evangelical upsurge are in the United States, from which the missionaries first went out. But it is very important to understand that, virtually everywhere and emphatically in Latin America, this new Evangelicalism is thoroughly indigenous and no longer dependent on support from U.S. fellow believers— indeed, Latin American Evangelicals have been sending missionaries to the Hispanic community in this country, where there has been a comparable flurry of conversions.

Needless to say, the religious contents of the Islamic and Evangelical revivals are totally different. So are the social and political consequences (of which I will say more later). But the two developments also differ in another very important respect: The Islamic movement is occurring primarily in countries that are already Muslim or among Muslim emigrants (as in Europe), while the Evangelical movement is growing dramatically throughout the world in countries where this type of religion was previously unknown or very marginal.

Exceptions to the Desecularization Thesis

Let me, then, repeat what I said a while back: The world today is massively religious, is *anything but* the secularized world that had been predicted (whether joyfully or despondently) by so many analysts of modernity. There are, however, two exceptions to this proposition, one somewhat unclear, the other very clear.

The first apparent exception is Europe—more specifically, Europe west of what used to be called the Iron Curtain (the developments in the formerly Communist countries are as yet very under-researched and unclear). In Western Europe, if nowhere else, the old secularization theory would seem to hold. With increasing modernization there has been an increase in key indicators of secularization, both on the level of expressed beliefs (especially those that could be called orthodox in Protestant or Catholic terms) and, dramatically, on the level of church-related behavior—attendance at services of worship, adherence to church-dictated codes of personal behavior (especially with regard to sexuality, reproduction, and marriage), recruitment to the clergy. These phenomena, long observed in the northern countries of the continent, have since World War II rapidly engulfed the south. Thus

Italy and Spain have experienced a rapid decline in church-related religion. So has Greece, thereby undercutting the claim of Catholic conservatives that Vatican II is to be blamed for the decline. There is now a massively secular Euro-culture, and what has happened in the south can be simply described (though not thereby explained) by that culture's invasion of these countries. It is not fanciful to predict that there will be similar developments in Eastern Europe, precisely to the degree that these countries too will be integrated into the new Europe.

While these facts are not in dispute, a number of recent works in the sociology of religion, notably in France, Britain, and Scandinavia, have questioned the term "secularization" as applied to these developments. A body of data indicates strong survivals of religion, most of it generally Christian in nature, despite the widespread alienation from the organized churches. A shift in the institutional location of religion, then, rather than secularization, would be a more accurate description of the European situation. All the same, Europe stands out as quite different from other parts of the world, and certainly from the United States. One of the most interesting puzzles in the sociology of religion is why Americans are so much more religious *as well as* more churchly than Europeans.

The other exception to the desecularization thesis is less ambiguous. There exists an international subculture composed of people with Western-type higher education, especially in the humanities and social sciences, that is indeed secularized. This subculture is the principal "carrier" of progressive, Enlightened beliefs and values. While its members are relatively thin on the ground, they are very influential, as they control the institutions that provide the "official" definitions of reality, notably the educational system, the media of mass communication, and the higher reaches of the legal system. They are remarkably similar all over the world today, as they have been for a long time (though, as we have seen, there are also defectors from this subculture, especially in the Muslim countries). Again, regrettably, I cannot speculate here as to why people with this type of education should be so prone to secularization. I can only point out that what we have here is a globalized *elite* culture.

In country after country, then, religious upsurges have a strongly populist character. Over and beyond the purely religious motives, these are movements of protest and resistance *against* a secular elite. The so-called culture war in the United States emphatically shares this feature. I may observe in passing that the plausibility of secularization theory owes much to this international subculture. When intellectuals travel, they usually touch down in intellectual circles—that is, among people much like themselves. They can easily fall into the misconception that these people reflect the overall visited society, which, of course, is a big mistake. Picture a secular intellectual from Western Europe socializing with colleagues at the faculty club of the University of Texas. He may think he is back home. But then picture him trying to drive through the traffic jam on Sunday morning in downtown Austin—or, heaven help him, turning on his car radio! What happens then is a severe jolt of what anthropologists call culture shock.

RESURGENT RELIGION: ORIGINS AND PROSPECTS

After this somewhat breathless *tour d'horizon* of the global religious scene, let me turn to some the questions posed for discussion in this set of essays. *First, what are the origins of the worldwide resurgence of religion?* Two possible answers have already been mentioned. One: Modernity tends to undermine the taken-for-granted certainties by which people lived through most of history. This is an uncomfortable state of affairs, for many an intolerable one, and religious movements that claim to give certainty have great appeal. Two: A purely secular view of reality has its principal social location in an elite culture that, not surprisingly, is resented by large numbers of people who are not part of it but who feel its influence (most troublingly, as their children are subjected to an education that ignores or even directly attacks their own beliefs and values). Religious movements with a strongly anti-secular bent can therefore appeal to people with resentments that sometimes have quite non-religious sources.

But I would refer once more to the little story with which I began, about American foundation officials worried about "fundamentalism." In one sense, there is nothing to explain here. Strongly felt religion has always been around; what needs explanation is its absence rather than its presence. Modern secularity is a much more puzzling phenomenon than all these religious explosions—if you will, the University of Chicago is a more interesting topic for the sociology of religion than the Islamic schools of Qom. In other words, the phenomena under consideration here on one level simply serve to demonstrate continuity in the place of religion in human experience.

Second, what is the likely future course of this religious resurgence? Given the considerable variety of important religious movements in the contemporary world, it would make little sense to venture a global prognosis. Predictions, if one dares to make them at all, will be more useful if applied to much narrower situations. One prediction, though, can be made with some assurance: There is no reason to think the world of the twenty-first century will be any less religious than the world is today. A minority of sociologists of religion have been trying to salvage the old secularization theory by what I would call the last-ditch thesis: Modernization *does* secularize, and movements like the Islamic and the Evangelical ones represent last-ditch defenses by religion that cannot last; eventually, secularity will triumph—or, to put it less respectfully, eventually Iranian mullahs, Pentecostal preachers, and Tibetan lamas will all think and act like professors of literature at American universities. I find this thesis singularly unpersuasive.

Having made this general prediction—that the world of the next century will not be less religious than the world of today—I will have to speculate very differently regarding different sectors of the religious scene. For example, I think that the most militant Islamic movements will find it hard to maintain their present stance *vis-à-vis* modernity once they succeed in taking over the governments of their countries (this, it seems, is already happening in Iran). I also think that Pentecostalism, as it exists today among mostly poor and uneducated people, is unlikely to retain its present religious and moral characteristics unchanged, as many of these people experience upward social mobility (this has already been observed extensively in the United States). Generally, many of these religious movements are linked to non-religious forces of one sort or another, and the future course of the former will be at least partially determined by the course of the latter. In the United States, for instance, militant Evangelicalism will have a different future course if some of its causes succeed in the political and legal arenas than if it continues to be frustrated in these arenas. Also, in religion as in every other area of human endeavor, individual personalities play a much larger role than most social scientists and historians are willing to concede. There might have been an Islamic revolution in Iran without the Ayatollah Khomeini, but it would probably have looked quite different. No one can predict the appearance of charismatic figures who will launch powerful religious movements in unexpected places. Who knows—perhaps the next religious upsurge in America will occur among disenchanted postmodernist academics!

Third, do the resurgent religions differ in their critique of the secular order? Yes, of course they do, depending on their particular belief

71

systems. Cardinal Ratzinger and the Dalai Lama will be troubled by different aspects of contemporary secular culture. What both will agree upon, however, is the shallowness of a culture that tries to get along without any transcendent points of reference. And they will have good reasons to support this view The religious impulse, the quest for meaning that transcends the restricted space of empirical existence in this world, has been a perennial feature of humanity (This is not a theological statement but an anthropological one—an agnostic or even an atheist philosopher may well agree with it.) It would require something close to a mutation of the species to extinguish this impulse for good. The more radical thinkers of the Enlightenment and their more recent intellectual descendants hoped for something like this, of course. So far it has not happened, and as I have argued, it is unlikely to happen in the foreseeable future. The critique of secularity common to all the resurgent movements is that human existence bereft of transcendence is an impoverished and finally untenable condition.

To the extent that secularity today has a specifically modern form (there were earlier forms in, for example, versions of Confucianism and Hellenistic culture), the critique of secularity also entails a critique of at least these aspects of modernity. Beyond that, however, different religious movements differ in their relation to modernity. As I have said, an argument can be made that the Islamic resurgence strongly tends toward a negative view of modernity; in places it is downright anti-modern or counter-modernizing, as in its view of the role of women. By contrast, I think it can be shown that the Evangelical resurgence is positively modernizing in most places where it occurs, clearly so in Latin America. The new Evangelicals throw aside many of the traditions that have been obstacles to modernization—machismo, for one, and also the subservience to hierarchy that has been endemic to Iberian Catholicism. Their churches encourage values and behavior patterns that contribute to modernization. To take just one important case in point: In order to participate fully in the life of their congregations, Evangelicals will want to read the Bible; this desire to read the Bible encourages literacy and, beyond this, a positive attitude toward education and self-improvement. They also will want to be able to join in the discussion of congregational affairs, since those matters are largely in the hands of laypersons (indeed, largely in the hands of women); this lay operation of churches necessitates training in administrative skills, including the conduct of public meetings and the keeping of financial accounts. It is not fanciful to suggest that in this way Evangelical congregations serve—inadvertently, to be sure—as schools for democracy and for social mobility.

RELIGIOUS RESURGENCE AND WORLD AFFAIRS

Other questions posed for discussion in this volume concern the relation of the religious resurgence to a number of issues not linked to religion.

■ First, *international politics.* Here one comes up head-on against the thesis, eloquently proposed not long ago by Samuel Huntington, that, with the end of the Cold War, international affairs will be affected by a "clash of civilizations" rather than by ideological conflicts. There is something to be said for this thesis. The great ideological conflict that animated the Cold War is certainly dormant for the moment, but I, for one, would not bet on its final demise. Nor can we be sure that new ideological conflicts may not arise in the future. To the extent that nationalism is an ideology (more accurately, each nationalism has its *own* ideology), ideology is alive and well in a long list of countries.

It is also plausible that; in the absence of the overarching confrontation between Soviet Communism and the American-led West, cultural animosities suppressed during the Cold War period are surfacing. Some of these animosities have themselves taken on an ideological form, as in the assertion of a distinctive Asian identity by a number of governments and intellectual groups in East and Southeast Asia. This ideology has become especially visible in debates over the allegedly ethnocentric/Eurocentric character of human rights as propagated by the United States and other Western governments and governmental organizations. But it would probably be an exaggeration to see these debates as signaling a clash of civilizations. The situation closest to a religiously defined clash of civilizations would come about if the world-view of the most radical branches of the Islamic resurgence came to be established within a wider spectrum of countries and became the basis of the foreign policies of these countries. As yet this has not happened.

To assess the role of religion in international politics, it would be useful to distinguish between political movements that are genuinely inspired by religion and those that use religion as a convenient legitimation for political agendas based on quite non-religious interests. Such a distinction is difficult but not impossible. Thus there is no reason to doubt that the suicide bombers of the Islamic Haws movement truly believe in the religious motives they avow. By contrast, there is good

73

reason to doubt that the three parties involved in the Bosnian conflict, commonly represented as a clash between religions, are really inspired by religious ideas. I think it was P. J. O'Rourke who observed that these three parties are of the same race, speak the same language, and are distinguished only by their religion, which none of them believe. The same skepticism about the religious nature of an allegedly religious conflict is expressed in the following joke from Northern Ireland: As a man walks down a dark street in Belfast, a gunman jumps out of a doorway, holds a gun to his head, and asks, "Are you Protestant or Catholic?" The man stutters, "Well, actually, I'm an atheist." "Ah yes," says the gunman, "but are you a Protestant or a Catholic atheist?"

■   Second, *war and peace.* It would be nice to be able to say that religion is everywhere a force for peace. Unfortunately, it is not. Very probably religion in the modern world more often fosters war, both between and within nations. Religious institutions and movements are fanning wars and civil wars on the Indian subcontinent, in the Balkans, in the Middle East, and in Africa, to mention only the most obvious cases. Occasionally, indeed, religious institutions try to resist Warlike policies or to mediate between conflicting parties. The Vatican mediated successfully in some international disputes in Latin America. There have been religiously inspired peace movements in several countries (including the United States, during the Vietnam War). Both Protestant and Catholic clergy have tried to mediate the conflict in Northern Ireland, though with notable lack of success.

But it is probably a mistake to look here simply at the actions of formal religious institutions or groups. There may be a diffusion of religious values in a society that could have peace-prone consequences even in the absence of formal actions by church bodies. For example, some analysts have argued that the wide diffusion of Christian values played a mediating role in the process that ended the apartheid regime in South Africa, even though the churches were mostly polarized between the two sides of the conflict, at least until the last few years of the regime, when the Dutch Reformed Church reversed its position on apartheid.

■   Third, *economic development.* The basic text on the relation of religion and economic development is, of course, the German sociologist Max Weber's 1905 work *The Protestant Ethic and the Spirit of Capitalism.* Scholars have been arguing over the thesis of this book for over ninety years. However one comes out on this (I happen to be an unreconstructed Weberian), it is clear that some values foster modern economic development more than others. Something *like* Weber's "Protestant ethic" is probably functional in an early phase of capitalist growth—an ethic, whether religiously inspired or not, that values personal discipline, hard work, frugality, and a respect for learning. The new Evangelicalism in Latin America exhibits these values in virtually crystalline purity, so that my own mental subtitle for the research project on this topic conducted by the center I direct at Boston University has been, "Max Weber is alive and well and living in Guatemala." Conversely, Iberian Catholicism, as it was established in Latin America, clearly does *not* foster such values.

But religious traditions can change. Spain experienced a remarkably successful period of economic development beginning in the waning years of the Franco regime, and one of the important factors was the influence of Opus Dei, which combined rigorous theological orthodoxy with a market-friendly openness in economic matters. I have suggested that Islam, by and large, has difficulties with a modern market economy; yet Muslim emigrants have done remarkably well in a number of countries (for instance, in sub-Saharan Africa), and there is a powerful Islamic movement in Indonesia that might yet play a role analogous to that of Opus Dei in the Catholic world. I should add that for years now there has been an extended debate over the part played by Confucian-inspired values in the economic success stories of East Asia; if one is to credit the "post-Confucian thesis" and also to allow that Confucianism is a religion, then here would be a very important religious contribution to economic development.

One morally troubling aspect of this matter is that values functional at one period of economic development may not be functional at another. The values of the "Protestant ethic" or a functional equivalent thereof are probably essential during the phase that Walt Rostow called "the take-off," but may not be so in a later phase. Much less austere values may be more functional in the so-called post-industrial economies of Europe, North America, and East Asia. For example, frugality, however admirable from a moral viewpoint, may actually be a vice economically speaking. Although undisciplined hedonists have a hard time climbing out of primitive poverty, they can do well in the high-tech, knowledge-driven economies of the advanced societies.

■   Finally, *human rights and social justice.* Religious institutions have, of course, made many statements on human rights and social justice. Some of these have had important political consequences, as in the civil-rights struggle in the United States and the collapse of

75

Communist regimes in Europe. But, as mentioned previously, there are different religiously articulated views about the nature of human rights. The same goes for ideas about social justice: what is justice to some groups is gross injustice to others. Sometimes it is very clear that positions taken by religious groups on such matters are based on a religious rationale; the principled opposition to abortion and contraception by the Roman Catholic Church is such a clear case. At other times, though, positions on social justice, even if legitimated by religious rhetoric, reflect the location of the religious functionaries in this or that network of non-religious social classes and interests. To stay with the same example, I think that this is the case with most of the positions taken by American Catholic institutions on social-justice issues other than those relating to sexuality and reproduction.

I have dealt very briefly with immensely complex matters. I was asked to give a global overview, and that is what I have tried to do. There is no way that I can end this with some sort of uplifting sermon. Both those who have great hopes for the role of religion in the affairs of this world and those who fear this role must be disappointed by the factual evidence. In assessing this role, there is no alternative to a nuanced, case-by-case approach. But one statement can be made with great confidence: Those who neglect religion in their analyses of contemporary affairs do so at great peril.

4

Culture and Socioeconomic Change

As mentioned in Chapter 1 above, Peter L. Berger founded the Institute for the Study of Economic Culture (ISEC) at Boston University in 1985, four years after he took up an appointment as professor of sociology there. As he cryptically notes in his career memoir, *Adventures of an Accidental Sociologist* (2011: 207), "Later on, for uninteresting reasons having to do with the interests of donors, we changed the name twice—first to Institute on Religion and World Affairs (IRWA), then to Institute on Culture, Religion and World Affairs (CURA)."

Despite the name changes, the agenda of the institute has remained the same. Broadly speaking, its objective is to furnish with the help of sociological research practically applicable insights into the relationship between socioeconomic change and culture, in the sense of beliefs, values, and lifestyles. CURA uses its ample financial resources—Peter L. Berger has always been a very successful fund-raiser—not only for research activities but also for colloquia and conferences with decision-makers and consortia. It frequently manages to procure grants by promising funders that the research findings will be disseminated beyond the narrow confines of science and will be fed into public debate. Another defining characteristic of the way the institute works is its global perspective, which is assured by the close collaboration between the experts in CURA's international network.

4.1 Economic Culture

The institute's profile stems not least from Berger's humanitarian drive to search for answers to global development problems. These problems have been on his agenda since the 1960s. In numerous publications, he developed more and more detailed insights into the manifold causes of poverty and under-development. Milestones include *The Homeless Mind* (1973a), which analyzed the impact of modernization on the

Third World; *Pyramids of Sacrifice* (1974a), which dealt with political ethics as applied to social change in the Third World; and *The Capitalist Revolution* (1986a), in which Berger coined the term economic culture to denote one focus of CURA's research. Over the years, Berger developed a firm, empirically grounded stance on the chances of, and barriers to, modernization and economic prosperity. He arrived at the conviction that the improvement of the material living conditions of large numbers of people could succeed only with a capitalist model of development (cf. 2011: 142). He pointed out that socialist models of development had been discredited because they had improved only the material standard of living of the ruling elite (cf. 1992a: 10).[1]

Because the economy, politics, and culture are closely linked, Berger views economic and political liberalization as two interwoven processes whose relationship is, however, an asymmetrical one. He argues (e.g., 1986a) that, although capitalism is a necessary condition of democracy, the converse is by no means the case. China is not the only example that clearly shows that market liberalization in authoritarian systems with limited fundamental political rights or in totalitarian systems can give rise to an enormous economic boom. Successful capitalism releases democratic forces whose dynamism is hard to subdue even with massive effort. However, as Berger emphasizes with reference to China: "Whether these forces inexorably lead to democracy is another question" (1997c).

With the concept of economic culture, Berger refers to the way in which economic arrangements interact with other processes in society. In *The Capitalist Revolution* (1986a), he stresses that:

> The phrase *economic culture* . . . does not refer to some mysterious, empirically inaccessible element. Quite simply, it denotes the sociocultural context within which economic activities and economic institutions exist. It points to a certain set of relationships; it does *not* imply a theory of these relationships. Thus, to speak of economic culture by no means implies that culture always determines economics, or even that cultural factors must be taken into account in all phenomena that an economist studies. Whether culture does or does not enter into the explanation of any economic situation must always be a matter of empirical inquiry. (1986a: xx)

Their shared assumption of the fundamental cultural impact of globalization formed the starting point for a large-scale project spanning ten countries that Berger codirected with Samuel P. Huntington in the

1990s. This cross-national comparative study revealed that the widely held notion of a dominant, *monolithic* global culture was untenable. In an essay entitled the "Four Faces of Global Culture," (1997d: 23–29), Berger proposes that global culture has at least four faces. He distinguishes typologically four simultaneous processes of cultural globalization: "First is what Huntington nicely calls the 'Davos culture' (after the annual World Economic Summit that meets in that Swiss luxury resort)." The participants in this culture are the political and economic elite. Berger calls the second grouping the "faculty club culture": "Essentially this is the internationalization of the Western intelligentsia, its values and ideologies." The third process of cultural globalization is popular culture: "Here Barber's term 'McWorld' fits best. And it is this culture that is most credibly subsumed under the category of Westernization." And "fourthly, yet perhaps not finally," Berger recognizes in Evangelical Protestantism, especially in its Pentecostal version, the fourth face of global culture. What these four faces have in common is their Western provenance.

The papers from the project were published in a book entitled *Many Globalizations: Cultural Diversity in the Contemporary World* (Berger & Huntington 2002b). In the chapter that she contributed to the book, country researcher Tulasi Srinivas (2002b: 89–90) takes Berger's western-centric "Four Faces" essay as her starting point and examines cultural globalization as a *two*-way process. She focuses on non-Western, primarily Indian, contributions to the process of cultural globalization, arguing that: "While cultural globalization forces do enter India, cultural models are also increasingly emitted *from* India." In his recent career memoir, Berger (2011: 239) acknowledges that these counter-emissions are, indeed, "important countervailing cultural forces": "Some come from Latin America (salsa music), some from Africa ('Mandela shirts'). But the major ones come from Asia. Some may be deemed superficial, like the consumption of sushi or curry dishes. . . . Others are clearly more existentially significant, like martial arts or so-called spirituality."

The country-specific tableaux of cultural globalization presented in *Many Globalizations* (Berger & Huntington 2002b) reveal the complexity of the cultural dynamics of globalization. In his introduction to the book, Berger highlights a number of key aspects. They include:

1. *Individuation*: "If there is one theme that all have in common, it is individuation: all sectors of the emerging global culture enhance the

independence of the individual over against tradition and collectivity" (ibid., 9).

2. *Localization* in the sense of "significant local modifications" of the global culture (ibid., 10).
3. *Hybridization* as "the deliberate effort to synthesize foreign and native cultural traits" (loc. cit.). Berger cites Japan as a most successful pioneer of this response to globalization.
4. *Alternative globalizations*—"that is, cultural movements with a global outreach originating outside the Western world and indeed impacting on the latter" (ibid., 12). And finally,
5. *Subglobalizations*—to wit, "movements with a regional rather than a global reach that nevertheless are instrumental in connecting the societies on which they impinge with the emerging global culture. 'Europeanization' is probably the most important case of this. . . ." (ibid., 14).

4.2 Neo-Weberianism

Berger owes his appreciation of the immense importance of culture for economic development to Max Weber. Indeed, he describes the agenda of CURA and its predecessors as "neo-Weberian" (2011: 209). The research projects conducted under the auspices of CURA are extremely diverse. They include, for example, studies on Pentecostalism in Latin America and South Africa, on the relationship to democracy of the Russian Orthodox Church, and on the political and economic implications of morals and ethics. However, all these projects have one theme in common, namely the elective affinity between culture (including religious values and convictions) and economic, political, and civil society development.

In his famous treatise *The Protestant Ethic and the Spirit of Capitalism* (2003 [1904/5]), Weber argues that the Protestant ethic—characterized by inner-worldly asceticism and a calling to worldly duties—had been a factor in the genesis of capitalism in the Western world; that this ethic could not be understood without reference to its roots in Protestant dogmatism; and that Calvinism and the Baptist sects had been independent carriers of this process.[2]

According to Martin Endress (2007: 50–51), Weber's hypothesis of the link between Protestantism and capitalism contains the following three "argumentative steps": In the course of the search in everyday life for signs of orientation with regard to the other world, the Protestant work ethic leads to a reinterpretation of the religious guiding principle on the part of the adherents, the majority of whom just coincidentally happen to belong to the commercial *bourgeoisie*.

A pragmatic logic of the profitability of action is generated, which leads to the establishment of a permanent competitive situation. In the context of social groupings (sects), the doctrine of predestination encourages the systematic and mutual observation of the adherents to see who has been elected by the grace of God to be saved. As divine salvation has been institutionalized as the ultimate goal in life, they all want to be perceived as members of the elect. Wealth, or being well-to-do, is considered a sign that the person in question is a member of the elect. For this reason, the originally "anti-active character" of the doctrine of predestination is reversed. This reinterpretation creates permanent competition among the members of the group with regard to the knowledge that one belongs to the elect and to the honor of being recognized within the community as a person in possession of the grace of God: "Material wealth 'functions' as a sign of success and a symbol of being among the elect when it is invested with permanence—that is, when it is combined with an ascetic lifestyle that is geared toward relentless toil and the accumulation of wealth, thereby leading to a systematization of the entire conduct of life" (ibid., 51; our translation).

This sociological interpretation appears only at first glance to contradict the view taken by Weber in *The Protestant Ethic* (2003 [1904/5]: 104) that the Calvinist doctrine had evoked individualism in the sense of "the feeling of unprecedented inner loneliness"—a view that he impressively substantiated with recourse to Puritanical literature from the sixteenth and seventeenth centuries. In Chapter II of *The Protestant Ethic*, which is devoted to "The Spirit of Capitalism," Weber postulates that: "In order that a manner of life so well adapted to the peculiarities of capitalism could be selected at all, i.e. should come to dominate others, it had to originate somewhere, and not in isolated individuals alone, but as a way of life common to whole *groups* of men" (ibid., 55; emphasis added).

The classical sociology-of-knowledge content of Weber's studies in the sociology of religion lies in references to specific groups of carriers. For example, in Note 36 to Chapter IV of *The Protestant Ethic* (ibid., 226), he contradicts the widely held view that predestination was merely a dogma of theologians rather than a popular doctrine. Following Koehler, he argues that the "masses (meaning the *petite bourgeoisie* of Holland) were thoroughly imbued with predestination." Hence, the dogma of predestination was what the sociology of knowledge calls "commonsense knowledge" (1966a: 15) and had, therefore, to be endured on a large scale. In the main text (p. 110), Weber points out that "for the broad mass of ordinary men . . . the *certitudo salutis* in the sense of the recognizability of the state of grace necessarily became of absolutely dominant importance." By contrast, the question: "Am I one of the elect?" did not plague those whom Weber (1978 [1922]: 538) calls "religious virtuosis." Calvin, for example, "felt himself to be the chosen agent of the Lord, and was certain of his own salvation" (Weber 2003 [1904/5]: 110).

According to Berger, the postulated connection between (inner-worldly, ascetic) Protestantism and capitalism—which Weber does not, of course, perceive as causal but rather as one of elective affinity—is historically correct. However, he argues that the constituent elements of the cultural package "Protestant ethic" that Weber put together can be dismantled and detached from their religious base. These elements comprise a morally laden work ethic, a rational worldview devoid of magic, a systematic, disciplined conduct of life (what Weber called "life-discipline"), disciplined consumption in the sense of delayed gratification, and a consuming interest in education (2004b). Examples of "this-worldly asceticism" and a systematic, controlled conduct of life, in particular, can also be found without a Protestant basis. In the early phase of economic development, at any rate, they prove to be functional attitudes and habits—irrespective of how they are religiously or ethically justified.[3]

To put it simply: Individuals engage in business and rise out of poverty. Eventually they themselves, or the next generation, move up to the middle class. After some time, a community with such focused people boasts successful economic development. Individual entrepreneurial thinking and action are necessary, but not sufficient, conditions because development can be massively impaired by macro-economic, political, and ecological circumstances—that is, trade restrictions, abuse of power, or lack of resources. According to Berger, Weber was particularly mistaken in his assumption that Confucianism was inherently non-conducive to capitalism. The rise of the four Little Tigers—South Korea, Taiwan, Hong Kong, and Singapore—is a striking illustration not only of the way a Confucian culture acts as a driving force for capitalism but also of the importance of culture for economic development. The latter insight was alien to neo-Marxist theory in the early 1980s.

4.3 CURAtorium

Under the auspices of CURA and its predecessors, and within the framework of the institute's neo-Weberian agenda, Peter L. Berger and his many collaborators have tilled a number of hitherto largely fallow fields. The institute's studies on Pentecostalism can certainly be described as pioneering. Berger (2011: 32) recognized earlier than most the "veritable tsunami of Pentecostal Christianity sweeping across Latin America, sub-Saharan Africa, parts of Asia, and other unlikely places." Hence, when founding ISEC in 1985, he decided to make Pentecostal studies an important part of the institute's agenda, and he continues actively to promote research in this area.

Berger's acknowledgement of the erroneous nature of secularization theory is therefore empirically underpinned. Well-nigh explosive outbursts of religious fervor can be observed throughout the world—in all the major religions, and, as a rule, in a creative synthesis with folk beliefs, as illustrated by the mixing of charismatic Christianity and indigenous African religions.

However, the range of research topics covered by the institute is by no means limited to themes such as Pentecostalism, Eastern Christian Orthodoxy's relation to democracy in Russia, or the quantitative increase in the well-educated Evangelical middle class in America. The latest fruit of its projects on Eurosecularity is the book *Religious America — Secular Europe?* (Berger et al. 2008b). Moreover, for many years now, intensive research on Islam has been conducted under its auspices. The latter studies have focused not only, but especially, on moderate and fundamentalist tendencies. The focus of studies on China, Hong Kong, and Taiwan has been on civil-society aspects. Furthermore, a CURA project entitled *"Between Relativism and Fundamentalism,"* which attempted to identify a middle position from the perspective of Christian and Jewish traditions, yielded, among other things, *In Praise of Doubt: How to Have Convictions Without Becoming a Fanatic* (2009), a book that Berger coauthored with Anton Zijderveld (see Chapter 6 below).

The strongly empirically oriented research program of CURA and its predecessors, which has been outlined only roughly here, has not yet yielded a differentiated theory of the relationship between culture and socioeconomic change. However, in "Faith and Development: A global perspective" (2008d: 10–11), a lecture he delivered in Johannesburg in 2008, Berger draws five conclusions from the institute's research:

- "The first is that religious traditions are malleable. . . . No tradition is carried through history as an inert entity.
- "Second, the socioeconomic potential of the religious tradition may be latent for long periods of time until triggered by some new set of circumstances. Confucianism presents us with such a case.

- "Third, the socioeconomic effects of a religious tradition typically have an expiration date. In other words, these effects may not only be latent, but are likely to be perishable once they have become manifest.
- "Fourth, economic development is typically initiated by a vanguard.
- "Fifth, modernity can come in different forms. . . ."

He goes on to point out that "there are certain attitudes and habits without which modernity cannot arise or persist. Broadly speaking, these are the rational mindsets and behavior patterns without which modern science, technology, and bureaucratic administration cannot exist. . . . I have called these the intrinsic features of modernity."

Notes

1. This publication was followed by a series of edited volumes including *Modern Capitalism* (Vol. 1): *Capitalism and Equality in America* (1987a); *Modern Capitalism* (Vol. 2): *Capitalism and Equality in the Third World* (1987b); *The Capitalist Spirit: Towards a Religious Ethic of Wealth Creation* (1990).
2. According to Weber (op. cit.: 144), Pietism and Methodism are not independent sources of Protestant asceticism but merely "secondary movements" and weaker versions of the ascetic ethic of Puritanism in Holland and England.
3. Berger argues that inner-worldly asceticism is functional only in the early stage of economic development. In later stages it can even prove to be dysfunctional. The systematic conduct of life is not necessarily conducive to knowledge work, for example. It is no longer necessary that every individual make an economically productive contribution. Rather, intellectual productivity is called for, which may be rooted in a different, unsystematic conduct of life (cf. 2004b).

Our Economic Culture

by Peter L. Berger

By economic culture, which is the name of our research center at Boston University, we mean the cultural context of economic activity. There is no hidden theory behind that term; we don't assume that culture determines economics or that economics determines culture. We simply delineate an empirical area of investigation. We've been in existence for seven years and we've done a lot of things in those seven years. I'm going to tell you about three areas that we explored.

There are about forty million Chinese outside the People's Republic and they constitute one of the great economic miracles of the 20th century. I have been very much intrigued with that phenomenon and almost inevitably, it seems to me, if one looks at that phenomenon, one asks the question of whether Chinese culture has anything to do with that success. What are the cultural resources these people have which may help to explain their success? We have a project in collaboration with the Business School of the University of Hong Kong (run by its dean, Gordon Redding) looking at the values, beliefs, life styles, and institutions of overseas Chinese business people. On one of my early visits to East Asia, in the mid seventies, I was in Taiwan and I talked to an economist, Shirley Kuo, who had written on a very interesting aspect of Taiwan economic development, which is that there is an "anti-Kuznets" effect in Taiwan. Contrary to the Kuznets thesis, at the time of greatest economic growth there was less inequality, specifically less income inequality. I talked to her about this, and she had various theories. She was then a professor of economics and later became head of the National Bank. She was going on and on, about the Gini coefficients and this and that, and I said to her, "Well Professor Kuo, you spent most of your professional life studying one of the great economic success stories of the 20th century—the story of Taiwan. Do you think that Chinese culture had anything to do with that success?" And she stopped as if I had asked an extremely curious question and thought for about a minute and then she said, "Yes, Chinese people work very hard." Then she stopped again, thinking, and then she went on talking about Gini coefficients. She had nothing else to say on the subject. Now, let me say this was a very intelligent person, a very good economist. She simply hadn't thought about this; it was irrelevant to her.

We've had this Hong Kong based project going for several years; one book has come out and several articles. I think I now have a pretty good idea of what makes for their success. I'm going to give you one major one. The absolutely central institution one has to add for the understanding of Chinese business is the Chinese family, the overseas Chinese family. This is very important and has all sorts of implications. One implication that we came upon, which was very interesting, is that it has something to do with the size and complexity of businesses where Chinese are successful—this is the precise opposite of what is true for the Japanese. In North America and Europe there has been a lot of discussion of an "Asian management style." There is no Asian management style; in fact Japanese and Chinese management are about as different from each other as two types of management can possibly be. The Japanese have shown an enormous ability to create very strong organizations of people who are not related to each other and to develop enormous loyalty to each other and to their organization. The Chinese are, you can say, unable or unwilling to do this. Chinese firms are almost always family firms. And what this implies is what some anthropologists have called the "threshold of trust," whom can you trust? And the traditional Chinese cultural answer is very simple—you can only trust close relatives; you can't trust anyone else. That leads to a very interesting problem. What if your firm is very successful and it grows and you put your close relatives in every important position, you continue to grow and you run out of close relatives. That is, you run out of people you can trust. What do you do then? The empirical answer is the firm splits and people go off in different directions. Now some don't. We interviewed some managers who were *not* family members. These were the most unhappy people we talked to because no one trusted them. They knew they weren't going to get anywhere, and the only thought they had in their mind was to go out as soon as possible and start their own business. The only way in which large firms seem to work with that kind of principle is if they have a very simple organization, in which case the firm may be large, but it does not require a lot of decision centers, so you can put your trusted relatives in those few positions. Shipping is a main example of this that we discovered.

Here we look at a national culture, which is very ancient, which has certain very specific characteristics, which interestingly enough did not have these social and economic consequences in the home country but resulted through migration, for which there are very good reasons. So the same values, life styles, and family loyalties which were prevalent in China itself over the last 200 years did not have the consequences we see in Hong Kong or in Taiwan, or for that matter in Boston or Philadelphia with overseas Chinese. In the new environment these very old values and life styles suddenly acquire a social and economic significance which they did not have before. Let me mention two terms that come out of this and then drop this particular story. One term I found myself using is "latent cultural factors," that is, they may be latent for a long time and then in a new environment suddenly acquire a new potency in terms of economic and social dynamism. The other term which we stole from the economists, but gave somewhat different meaning, is to speak of "comparative cultural advantage." If you look at the role of overseas Chinese, particularly in Southeast Asia, the term suggests itself. They have a comparative cultural advantage over other ethnic groups.

Now, some important points: It is not a value judgement to say that someone has a comparative advantage in terms of economic achievement. This is not to make a value judgement about their culture at all; it simply says it has these consequences. It also suggests it is a relative advantage; obviously not all Chinese are successful. It also suggests, and this is very important, it may be a temporary advantage. Conditions may change. Let me drop the Chinese for the moment and get to my second story.

One must be very careful, if one looks at culture, not to fall into what I have called the "ancient curse theory of history," which is that somewhere in the past, somebody uttered a curse, and then for centuries people are obliged to follow this. In the case of the Chinese you might say it's an ancient blessing: Go and make money. I don't think history works that way. Some cultural traits indeed survive over many centuries, though they may have different effects at different times, but culture also changes and sometimes, especially, in the modem world. There are dramatic and rapid cultural changes that occur. It is very important, if one is interested in this area of economics and culture, to look at such cases. One of the most dramatic cases in the world today, arguably the single most dramatic case (of which incidentally many people in North America and Europe have never heard, which is interesting) is the rapid spread of Evangelical Protestantism in the third world and especially most dramatically in Latin America. The idea that Latin America is a solidly Catholic continent is an obsolete idea. Latin America is rapidly producing a very sizable Protestant population. Guatemala, for reasons I don't claim to understand, has the highest percentage; it is now probably between 25 and 30 percent of the population. We've been interested particularly in looking at the social and economic consequences of this, which are formidable. We started out with an overview of the situation, and we've done two field studies (directed by David Martin of the London School of Economics) of new Protestant entrepreneurs in Chile and Brazil. My own mental subtitle of this project has been "Max Weber is alive and well and living in Santiago de Chile." As you look at these people and what they believe and how they live, it is as if they have stepped out of the history books describing the behavior of English and New England Protestants two hundred years ago, except that they speak Spanish and have a somewhat more colorful worship service. Most of this Protestantism is Pentecostal, which is interesting. What we are witnessing here, is a cultural revolution. There is no other way to describe it. You have millions of people, who almost overnight as a result of a religious conversion (a clearly a religious conversion that is not politics under a religious label), rapidly change their life style with very far reaching consequences. One could describe the changes in that life style in different ways. I've used the term "cultural revolution." One can also say it's a "women's movement." This religious movement is basically driven by women, which is very interesting. Most of the preachers, not all, but most of the preachers are still men. The missionaries and the organizers are mostly women—formidable women, and they domesticate their husbands. It can also be described in Latin American terms as an anti-machismo revolution, as if they had read Max Weber. These Protestant women say to their husbands: "You're going to stop drinking, you're going to stop gambling, you're going to stop having what in Mexico one calls a *casa chica*—a little house for the other woman around the corner—you're going to save money, you're going to take an interest in the education of the children." Well, the men either accept this and become good little Puritans, or the women kick them out and either stay without men or acquire good little Puritans as their new husbands. The effects of this are frankly what you would expect: These people have a significant comparative cultural advantage against their Catholic or religiously indifferent neighbors (or in Brazil against the Afro-Brazilian cults, which also are not terribly conducive to successful economic development).

Let me emphasize again that what I'm saying here is not a value judgement. I'm not saying that these people are better than their neighbors. Perhaps, to make this graphically clear, let me tell a story that happened in the sort of ambience of our family some twenty years ago when we spent a lot of time in Mexico and became acquainted with a whole clan that came out of the state of Puebla. The reason that we got to know these people is beside the point. One of these individuals, whose name I think was Pablo, came from this village. He moved to Mexico City and opened a tailor shop where he did alterations. It was a hole in the wall, where he worked very hard, ten hours a day, seven days a week, took care of his family and acquired a little money. One day he disappeared and didn't return for two weeks. What he had done, was to take all his savings, go to Acapulco, check into one of the best hotels, get himself two call girls, stay there for two weeks, and blow every peso he had made. Now, there was subsequently a debate over the moral issues involved in this act. Was this man irresponsible—to be condemned—or was he to be admired? I must confess that I was not quite clear where I would come out. I think there is something to be said for his point of view, but what one can also say as an empirically oriented person is that this is not a value system or life style conducive to economic success. I don't think Pablo will ever become a Protestant, and in fact I would almost say I hope not. But if Pablo ever became a Protestant and changed his life style, perhaps out of that hole in the wall might come one day a trouser factory employing a hundred people and selling a lot of trousers in North America.

We have also been very interested in changing corporate culture in the advanced industrial societies. The most geographically expansive study of changing corporate culture that we have done so far is a study in five countries, four West European countries and the United States—led by Hausfried Velluer of the University of Frankfurt. We were particularly interested in a phenomena which we thought we detected, and now I can say I'm quite sure it's there: A strange symbiosis between what in the United States has been called the counter-culture, or the cultural developments of the late sixties, and the business culture. In the 1970s there was an interesting but rather short debate in the United States over what some people called "the new class." This referred to a class of intellectuals, people working in the knowledge industry, who were supposed to be hostile to capitalism, hostile to business. In the late sixties and early seventies there was a lot to be said for this. That analysis was somewhat grandiloquently called "New Class Theory." It wasn't that much of a theory, but the idea has some empirical merit and is still worth exploring today. We started out by asking how business deals with this and how business culture responds to these significant cultural changes that have been taking place in western societies for the last twenty-five years. And what we came upon was unexpected. It was remarkable synthesis, a kind of symbiosis. Let me give you an example of this.

We did a conference at the conclusion of this study on what, in the United States, are called personal development programs. This is a kind of expansion of the notion of employee benefits in new directions such as child care, elder care, marriage counseling, even spiritual development where employees go on weekends where they meditate together. And we found this not only in the United States; we found it very much in Western Europe (e.g., Germany and Sweden). At this conference we had a man from Volvo who talked about Volvo's programs of personal development, of which he was very proud. I thought it was a totalitarian nightmare, but he was very proud. Here the corporation becomes (one is tempted to think of the papal encyclical, *Mater et Magistra)* a mother and teacher figure, embracing the employees in a kind of total embrace. Many of these ideas come from the late sixties, from the counter-culture: Self-realization, feminism, sensitivity, sensitivity to the environment, getting in touch with your own body. All of these things were counter-cultural themes and now they come back to haunt us from Volvo Corporation.

What does this say about business as a supposed defender of conservative values? One consulting firm in Germany gave us their entire curriculum, which is like a college catalog. They have been successful in getting large German corporations to run their executives through these programs. These go on over long weekends and include meditation, Japanese sword fighting, unbelievable stuff. These German capitalists go through all of this and emerge believing that they will be better human beings and better manufacturers of whatever they manufacture.

This makes another point: A comparative advantage could be a temporary advantage. The person who did the British part of the five-country study is a sociologist, Bernice Martin, who is the wife of the major investigator of the Latin American Protestant study, David Martin. She went along with him on some of the trips to Latin America so she was a bridge between the two studies. We had a final meeting of the research staff of the five-country study in Holland, one of the countries we studied. Some of us were somewhat depressed by what we found. One shouldn't make value judgements as a social scientist, but I may as well admit that I find much of this quite repulsive. At any rate, some of us were not very happy with the findings. We sat in a hotel, late in the evening and I turned to Bernice Martin and I said: "Look, could we, in terms of cultural change, sum up what you and David have been finding among these Latin American Protestants in the phrase 'Less fornication'?" (the term fornication here obviously covers a lot of pleasures, not just sex). And she said, "Yeah, one could." Then I said, "Look, couldn't one sum up *this* study in the phrase 'more fornication'? (as compared to an earlier type of Protestant ethic business culture)?" And they all agreed, "Yeah, one could."

The next question is what I feel is the sixty-four billion D-mark question: As this cultural symbiosis takes place in the West, is it going to make us more or less competitive internationally? My first inclination would be it would make us less competitive, because I think if you want a general sociological rule, you could put it in very scientific language: "The hard nosed bastard usually wins out"—and these sensitive, conscience ridden, feminized executives, 1 think, are going to lose out. That would have been my hypothesis. I'm much less sure now. Let me tell you a story. A few years ago I was asked to speak to a conference of Japanese business people in Osaka on some modest subject-I think it was the future of Asian capitalism—and I prepared this very carefully. I always prepare things very carefully, which was a mistake, because if you've ever been to a Japanese conference, nobody cares what you say and no one listens to you. It's the harmony of the meeting which is important. Anyway, I'd prepared this talk and I had an episode in it. I had read a book for my own edification at the time, on Roman history. And I came upon the following story that in the early days of the Roman republic, when Rome was constantly at war with these little Greek kingdoms in the south of Italy, an envoy of the Roman Senate was sent to one of the Greek courts. One has to imagine him as a sort of sturdy, early republican. He found himself at dinner next to an Epicurean philosopher who explained to him all through dinner that in his view the purpose of human life was happiness. The

Roman envoy had never heard such a thing before, he listened with great interest and the only comment he had at the conclusion of the dinner was this, "I hope that you will continue to have these beliefs as long as you are at war with us." I said to my Japanese audience, "If I were a Japanese businessman, looking at North America and Western Europe, I think I would say, 'I hope you will continue to hold these values as long as you are in competition with us.'" It was a few years ago when I told this story. I'm not so sure now. I may have been misled by my own sense of revulsion against this new business culture. I should have remembered what sociologists learn very early: If people define a situation as real it is real in its consequences. If people believe this stuff, maybe they do become more productive, and maybe all these weekends with meditation and getting in touch with your own body and talking to plants or whatever will make us more competitive. There is the additional question, "what will happen to the Japanese?" which is not at all clear, but I will leave it at that.

5

Knowledge and Reality

Knowledge and reality are the key terms of the theory for the sociology of knowledge that Peter L. Berger and Thomas Luckmann developed in *The Social Construction of Reality* (1966a). The authors proceed from the assumption that the historically evolved sociocultural world is the product of human activity; that as a result of its objectivation this product acts back dialectically upon its producer; and that it is internalized in the course of socialization, thereby acquiring the status of more or less taken-for-granted reality (ibid., 61). These three "dialectical moments"—*externalization, objectivation*, and *internalization*—correspond to essential characteristics of the social world, namely, "*Society is a human product. Society is an objective reality. Man is a social product*" (loc. cit.). The paradigm thus established has often been referred to as social constructivism, a label Berger (2011: 88) describes as "unfortunate."

Berger and Luckmann argue that knowledge is constitutive of the construction of objective and subjective reality. However, they stress that—within the frame of reference of the sociology of knowledge—knowledge refers not to theoretical thought, to "ideas," or ideology, but rather to "everything that passes for knowledge in society, . . . to what people 'know' as 'reality' in their everyday non-theoretical lives" (1966a: 15). In this way, the authors liberate the sociology of knowledge from its narrow focus on the epistemological problem of the relativity of scientific thought, and, at the same time, they lay the foundations for a new sociology of knowledge.

5.1 The Problem of Relativity

Berger and Luckmann develop their theory for the sociology of knowledge in explicit contradistinction to the relativity of thought in general and sociological thought in particular, which Max Scheler (1980) defined as the central problem of the sociology of knowledge, and to Karl Mannheim's focus on relationism. Although they consider the relativity of all ideas, values, and truths (including their own) to be a question that must be addressed, they argue that such questions are not part of the sociology of knowledge, but rather "properly belong to the methodology of the social sciences, an enterprise that belongs to philosophy" (1966a: 13). This is eminently summed up in Berger and Luckmann's often-quoted dictum: "To include epistemological questions concerning the validity of sociological knowledge in the sociology of knowledge is somewhat like trying to push a bus on which one is riding" (loc. cit.).

For this reason, they argue that epistemological questions should not be dealt with within the framework of the empirical discipline of sociology. Even though they acknowledge that the social determination of thought (including their own) is beyond dispute, they argue that the sociology of knowledge is not epistemology. This contrasts sharply with Mannheim's view. He would have preferred to change the discipline's name to sociological epistemology.[1]

Peter L. Berger considers methodologically controlled objectivity to be a way in which *sociology* can deal with the problem of relativity. In his view, objectivity is part of the scientific relevance structure to which sociologists, who always have a number of relevance structures at their disposal, can switch. As Berger and Kellner (1981: 62) argue, "The possibility of scientific objectivity is grounded in the multiplicity of relevance structures within consciousness." From this perspective, objectivity is not inherent in any particular facts. Rather, it is the result of a process in which the scientist brackets his own standpoint. According to Berger (2008a: 197), the objective validity criteria of the social sciences facilitate the development of a theory "regardless of the personal background of the scientist." The proximity of Berger's understanding of objectivity to Weber's postulate of value-free social science is evident. In *Sociology Reinterpreted* (1981: 52), Berger and Kellner argue that "when sociologists embark on their scientific inquiry, they must 'bracket' these values as much as possible—not, needless to say, in the sense of giving them up or trying to forget them, but in the sense of controlling the way in which these values might distort the sociological vision." However, the authors (ibid., 48–49) point out that there is more at issue here than the scientist's pious intention to be objective: "The scientific relevance structure brings with it a body of theoretical and empirical knowledge that must be taken into account in any particular interpretation." In other words, this involves "bringing the new-to-be interpreted phenomena into a meaningful relation with comparable phenomena previously interpreted by other sociologists" (loc. cit.).[2]

Thus, in contrast to Mannheim, the authors do not question the sociologist's existential determination (*Seinsgebundenheit*). Rather, they note that "Precisely by using the tools of the sociology of knowledge, one can demonstrate that, far from being 'freely suspended,' intellectuals constitute a collectivity (some would even say a class) with very specific interests—and, as with other people, these interests color their perceptions of society" (ibid., 65). However, Berger and Kellner share Mannheim's view that social scientists form a (reference) group or a community with a common relevance structure and stock of knowledge. The authors invoke the image of a "republic of scholars," whose citizenship one acquires when one becomes a scientist. Moreover, as one also retains one's citizenship of society and of various social groupings, one enjoys "dual citizenship" (ibid., 66).

However, Berger has never been quite able to understand that many sociologists consider this to be a problem. For him, value-freeness means that science has its own objective validity criteria independent of the scientist's personal background. In his view, this does not imply that scientists—as private individuals—may not have value judgments. However, for the duration of their scientific enterprise, the individual assessment of the phenomenon in question must be bracketed. Berger's attitude could be summed up as follows: The more aware the scientist is of his own value judgments, the better able he is to avoid unconsciously confounding them with his analysis.

In "Sociology and Freedom" (in 1977a: xviii), a speech he delivered when he was awarded an honorary doctorate by Loyola University in Chicago in 1970, Berger elaborates on value-freeness in two frames of reference, noting that "the statement about the value-freeness of sociology is methodological; the statement about the value-freeness of the sociologist is ethical." From a methodological viewpoint, Berger emphatically insists that the *discipline of sociology* must be value free, because "The moment the discipline ceases to be value-free in principle, it ceases to be science, and becomes nothing but ideology, propaganda, a part of the instrumentarium of political manipulation" (loc. cit.) From an ethical standpoint, on the other hand, he adamantly rejects value-freeness on the part of the *practitioner of the discipline*, the sociologist, who is not only a scientist but also a private individual. For Berger the moralist, this differentiation was particularly important in those days. At a time—1970—when sociology faculties were politically radicalized, the insistence on methodological value-freeness was an offensive act, a sign that he refused to allow himself to be pressurized by the *zeitgeist*-dominating "Movement." However, at that time, in particular, Berger was well known for taking a stance—not only theologically but also politically—against America's Vietnam policy. In his view, value-freeness and moral responsibility are equally justified—but each to its own time and in its own sphere, and in accordance with one's own moral standards.

In addition to the postulate of value-freeness, Berger is also committed to the methodological principle of falsifiability. Here, he follows Weber rather than Popper (cf. Berger 1986d: 233),[3] stressing that "I have always believed that all theorizing that occurs within the frame of reference of the social sciences must be open to empirical testing" (ibid., 229). While he admits that "there are elements of my sociology of knowledge that may be meta-theoretical," he stresses that he has "usually been careful to mark them off as such" (loc. cit.).

Berger's sociology of knowledge is shaped by Weber's notion of understanding (*Verstehen*). He aims to interpret the "certainties"—the ("relative-natural") worldviews—of actors and social groups *sine ira et studio*, without reservations, and without an enlightenment impetus. Berger developed a special sociology-of-knowledge-based research design within the framework of a project entitled "South Africa Beyond Apartheid" (SABA)—the first project he conducted at Boston University (1986–1988). At the time, South Africa was still paralyzed by the system of apartheid. Each member of the hand-picked team of American and South African researchers was assigned to one major political actor—a political party, a left- or right-wing movement, a resistance group, the business community, a church, a trade union, etc.—and given the task of identifying and analyzing its normative and cognitive definitions of reality, its vision for the future of the country, and the main strategies it was pursuing for the realization of this vision. In a second—reality-testing—interview (Berger & Godsell 1988a: 5), interviewees were confronted with inconsistencies in their respective cognitive maps, with the typical criticisms expressed by their opponents, and with humanitarian aspects.

The findings of the project were published under the title *A Future South Africa: Visions, Strategies and Realities* (Berger & Godsell 1988a). Today, the book is obviously more of historical value. But at the time of its publication, it met with a huge response from the public and from political circles both in America and South Africa. In his recent career memoir, Berger (2011: 188) recalls:

> After publication of the book, we received quite a few letters of protest. But not a single one protested what we had said about the party of the letter writer. The protests were all about what had been said about other parties, along the lines of "You were deceived about the real intention of these bastards!" I found this methodological validation very encouraging, and I have used similar analytic schemes since then.

Apart from proving the potential of the sociology of knowledge to analyze a socially virulent issue, the project delivered on the promise of the new sociology of knowledge to reconstruct the diverse constructions of reality as knowledge—that is, as certainties incorporated into plausibility structures.

5.2 A Theory for the Sociology of Knowledge

Although Peter L. Berger and Thomas Luckmann (1966a: 13ff.) advocate drawing a clear line between the sociology of knowledge and epistemology, the theory for the sociology of knowledge presented in *The Social Construction of Reality* is by no means characterized by a narrow disciplinary approach. On the contrary, the authors integrate Alfred Schutz's mundane phenomenology, Arnold Gehlen and Helmuth Plessner's philosophical anthropology, fundamental perspectives of the early Marx, and the social psychology of Charles Horton Cooley and George Herbert Mead into a concise theoretical formation. Moreover, they manage to combine in a comprehensive theory of social action two theoretical positions that were hitherto deemed incompatible—to wit, Durkheim's notion that society is a reality *sui generis,* and Weber's postulate that society is constructed by subjectively meaningful human activity (ibid., 17–18, 185).

Durkheim appears to have been a source of inspiration for Berger and Luckmann from the word go, as can be seen from their definition (1966a: 1) of reality as "a quality appertaining to phenomena that we recognize as being independent of our own volition (we cannot 'wish them away')." In *Montesquieu and Rousseau: Forerunners of Sociology* (1965 [1892]: 12), Durkheim notes that "The subject matter of science can consist only of things that have a stable nature of their own and are able to resist the human will." Although the focus of Berger and Luckmann's treatise is on the reality of everyday life, or, more precisely, on the "analysis of the knowledge that guides conduct in everyday life" (1966a: 19), they never lose sight of the multiple realities in which people live. Rather, they repeatedly outline situations in which "the continuity of everyday reality is interrupted by a problem" (ibid., 24–25, 102–3)—situations in which the unproblematic becomes problematic. In other words, as Helmuth Plessner notes in his preface to the German edition of *The Social Construction of Reality* (*Die Soziale Konstruktion der Wirklichkeit,* 1969), the authors do not focus narrowly on the construction of *social* reality. Following Alfred Schutz, they define knowledge as "the certainty that phenomena are real and that they possess specific characteristics" (1966a: 1), thereby underlining the broadness of their knowledge concept. The subject matter of the sociology of knowledge is knowledge, irrespective of whether it is based on experience, opinion, belief, imagination, etc. In contrast to epistemological and positivistic sociology-of-knowledge positions, what is decisive for Berger and Luckmann is not whether the knowledge in question is true, but whether it passes for knowledge in a particular society and is thus socially approved as true (cf. Schutz & Natanson 1982: 349). In the latter work (loc. cit.) we find a concept ("the relative natural conception of the world") that is very similar to what Scheler (1980: 74) calls the "*relative* natural worldview" (cf. also Berger & Luckmann 1966a: 8). Scheler (loc. cit.) notes that:

> to the relative natural worldview of a group subject . . . belongs whatever is generally 'given' to this group *without question* and every object and content of meaning within the structural forms 'given' without specific spontaneous acts, a givenness which is universally held and felt to be *unneedy and incapable of justification*. But precisely such objects and contents can be *entirely different* for different groups and for the same groups during various developmental stages.

This social relativity—in other words, the fact that "specific agglomerations of 'reality' and 'knowledge' pertain to specific social contexts" (Berger & Luckmann 1966a: 3)—justifies sociology's interest in a complex of themes that touches also on philosophical questions, and legitimates the existence of the sociology of knowledge. The empirical agenda of the sociology of knowledge, which derives from the aforementioned plurality of "agglomerations of 'reality' and 'knowledge,'" reveals that this sub-discipline cuts across sociological sub-disciplines that focus on just one concrete subject (for example, education, the family, or consumption). This is because the social relativity of reality and knowledge—a basic tenet of the sociology of knowledge—is inherent in all sociological problems. However, as Berger and Luckmann (ibid., 186) stress, not every empirical study needs an injection of a sociology-of-knowledge "angle". Indeed, "in many cases this would be unnecessary for the cognitive goal at which these studies aim" (loc. cit.).

The agenda for the sociology of knowledge formulated by Berger and Luckmann (ibid., 3) is not limited to *"the analysis of the social construction of reality."* Rather, the authors propose that the discipline of sociology be given a sociology-of-knowledge foundation: "In sum, our conception of the sociology of knowledge implies a specific conception of sociology in general" (ibid., 189).[4] They contend that the task of the sociology of knowledge is to "seek to understand the processes by which [human knowledge is developed, transmitted, and maintained in social situations, MP] in such a way that a taken-for-granted 'reality' congeals for the man in the street" (ibid., 3).

From a sociology-of-knowledge perspective, knowledge is constitutive of the construction of reality insofar as: "What is real is a matter of social definition, and the form this definition takes is what is deemed to be reality" (Knoblauch 2005: 156; our translation).[5] Hence, knowledge and reality are complementary terms, as are meaning and life-world. This differentiation is the key to understanding *The Social Construction of Reality* because the authors' category of knowledge is understandable only with recourse to meaning. Indeed, Knoblauch (2005: 155) argues that "It is no distortion of [Berger and Luckmann's, MP] ideas to describe knowledge as socially relevant, socially objectivated, and socially transmitted meaning." Berger and Luckmann's analysis seeks to understand the way in which this reality-defining knowledge develops through processes of habitualization, typification, institutionalization, legitimation, and socialization. These processes must be understood in their interdependence with the construction of reality based on the dialectic of externalization, objectivation, and internalization. In other words, they must be viewed in the context of the interrelationship between knowledge and activity. That is what Knoblauch (2005: 17) means when he describes this approach as an integrative sociology of knowledge.

Two apparently contradictory phenomenological insights are fundamental to this understanding of knowledge: (a) all knowledge is constituted in consciousness, and (b) most knowledge is socially derived. This apparent contradiction can be resolved with the help of Schutz's notion of typification. Typification denotes those processes of consciousness in which current experiences and actions are compared with remembered experiences and actions. In this way, the unknown is transformed into the known.[6] In its most general form, the constitution of meaning is therefore nothing more than relating something to something else.

However, as the correlate of our subjective experience, the life-world comprises not only our own experiences but also the experiences of others transmitted mainly through language, the typifying medium par excellence. Berger and Luckmann (1966a: 30–31) point out that "The reality of everyday life contains typificatory schemes in terms of which others are apprehended and 'dealt with' in face-to-face encounters. . . . The typificatory schemes entering into face-to-face situations are, of course, reciprocal." Alfred Schutz (Schutz & Natanson 1982: 13–14) notes that, because the individual's biographical situation in everyday life is always a historical situation:

> Only a very small part of my knowledge of the world originates within my personal experience. The greater part is socially derived, handed down to me by my friends, my parents, my teachers and the teachers of my teachers. I am taught not only how to define my environment . . ., but also how typical constructs have to be formed in accordance with the system of relevances accepted from the anonymous unified point of view of the in-group. This includes ways of life, methods of coming to terms with the environment, efficient recipes for the use of typical means for bringing about typical ends in typical situations.

Typifications are not only basic forms of knowledge. They are also the link between one's access to the social world, which, by definition, is always subjective, and its intersubjective validity (cf. Srubar 1979: 47).

Berger and Luckmann (1966a) acknowledge that the construction of reality is not a *creatio ex nihilo*, nor is it random. Rather, it must be understood as limited by the possibilities of the actor and the possibilities of the action. Hence, they combine Schutz's notion that all knowledge is grounded in subjective meaning with fundamental insights of philosophical anthropology furnished by Arnold Gehlen and Helmuth Plessner. Knoblauch (2005: 154) refers to Gehlen and Plessner's approach as "negative anthropology." This paradigm emphasizes human beings' instinctual deficiencies; the plasticity of their needs and wants; the biological world-openness of human existence, "which is, and always must be, transformed by the social order into a relative world-closedness"; and the separation of consciousness from bodily existence, that is, "eccentric positionality." These characteristics limit human action and the social construction of reality.

Berger and Luckmann (1966a) were convinced that a sociology of knowledge that narrowly equates knowledge with theoretical thinking, and concerns itself only with the problem of existential determination (*Seinsgebundenheit*), was wasting its potential, Hence, when developing their theory for the sociology of knowledge, they picked up and developed a thread spun by the early Marx, from whom "the sociology of knowledge derived its root proposition—that man's consciousness is determined by his social being" (ibid., 5–6). The thread in question is Marx's twin concepts of "substructure/superstructure" (*Unterbau/Ueberbau*). In the authors' view, later Marxism's (for example Lenin's) tendency to identify the substructure with economic structure, and to regard the superstructure as a direct reflection thereof, was a misrepresentation of Marx's thought—not least because it failed to recognize the dialectical character of the determination that Marx had in mind: "What concerned Marx was that human thought is founded in human activity ('labor in the widest sense of the word') and in the social relations brought about by that activity" (ibid., 6) . . . "The important point for a theoretical sociology of knowledge is the dialectic between knowledge and its social base" (ibid., 200, Note 56). This Marxian insight corresponds to what the authors (ibid., 66) call the "fundamental dialectic of society," which they elaborate on as follows:

> The important principle for our general considerations is that the relationship between knowledge and its social base is a dialectical one, that is, knowledge is a social product and knowledge is a factor in social change. (ibid., 87)

With the insight that society is a human product, Berger and Luckmann follow Marx and, especially, Helmuth Plessner (1982: 385), because the human world created by human hand becomes "second nature" for its producers.[7]

In *The Social Construction of Reality* (1966a), the authors supplement the concepts of "externalization" and "objectivation,"[8] which were derived from Marx, with the concept of "internalization," the "third moment" in the dialectical process of the construction of reality (ibid., 61). They acknowledge that the social-psychological presuppositions on which their analysis of the internalization process are based were greatly influenced by George Herbert Mead and the symbolic-interactionist school of American sociology (ibid., 17). The authors owe to Mead their insight into the dialectic of social structure and psychological reality. Mead posited that the individual experiences his identity in socially defined terms and these definitions become subjectively real to him. Hence, the self and identity are socially constructed. This Meadian notion is an integral part of Berger and Luckmann's theoretical edifice, and the symbolic-interactionist tradition of social psychology constitutes an important addition to the sociology of knowledge—whose orientation is, as a result, no longer exclusively phenomenological (cf. Berger 1973a).

Knowledge is, in a sense, the transmission belt of the social construction of reality.[9] Moreover, as Berger and Luckmann (1966a: 66) note:

> It "programs" the channels in which externalization produces the objective world. It objectifies this through language and the cognitive apparatus based on language, that is, it orders it into objects to be apprehended as reality. It is internalized again *as* objectively valid truth in the course of socialization. Knowledge about society is thus a *realization* in the double sense of the word, in the sense of apprehending the objectivated social reality, and in the sense of ongoingly producing this reality.

For this reason, before analyzing the role of knowledge in the fundamental dialectic of society, Berger and Luckmann—in their introduction to the book—provide an insight into their understanding of the tasks of the sociology of knowledge. This is followed, in Section I, by a phenomenological description of the "Foundations of Knowledge in Everyday Life." In Section II (1.a), they explain with recourse to philosophical anthropology why social order is an anthropological necessity. In Section II (1.b) they investigate the "Origins of Institutionalization." Their chronological, or biographical, starting point is not the socialized individual—not the individual who is "thrown into" a "socio-historical *a priori*" (Luckmann 1983: 109) and who has always been exposed to socialization and internalization—but rather the "solitary individual on the proverbial desert island who habitualizes his activity while he attempts to construct a canoe out of matchsticks" (Berger & Luckmann 1966a: 53). The decision in favor of this approach stems, first, from the necessity to present in linear form what is actually a dialectic process, and, second, from the fact that it is the only evident access to the world:

> The fact that even such a solitary individual, assuming that he has been formed as a self (as we would have to assume in the case of our

matchstick-canoe builder), will habitualize his activity in accordance with biographical experience of a world of social institutions preceding his solitude need not concern us at the moment. (ibid., 54)[10]

Here lie the origins of institutionalization, which occurs "whenever there is a reciprocal typification of habitualized actions by types of actors. Put differently, any such typification is an institution" (loc. cit.).

In Berger and Luckmann's concept of institutionalization, action and knowledge form a single entity. As points out, institutions represent patterns of action crystallized as "a typical sequence that is binding upon two or more actors," in which these actors participate as incumbents of roles.[11] These action patterns "detach themselves from the subjectivity of the producers and become objectivated elements of reality, which are realized in action and are rendered predictable by the typicality of the patterns of activity" Knoblauch (2005: 158; our translation). As soon as they are transmitted to the others, such patterns of activity confront not only the recipients but also—by a mirror effect—the producers of this institutional world as an objective reality. Hence, it is with the acquisition of historicity that institutions acquire objectivated character (Berger & Luckmann 1966a: 58).

"*Society is a human product. Society is an objective reality. Man is a social product*" (ibid., 61). The dialectic so succinctly expressed by Berger and Luckmann in this social-constructionist rule of three consists in the fact that the producer (of a social world) and the product (the produced social world) interact with each other: "The product acts back upon the producer" (loc. cit.). As mentioned above, the first two stages of this process are termed externalization and objectivation. The third, and final, stage is internalization, the process by which the social world is embodied in individual consciousness in the course of socialization.

Institutions—that is, crystallized and objectivated action patterns— are transmitted to others as practical knowledge, so to speak.[12] In other words, "The objectivated meanings of institutional activity are conceived of as 'knowledge' and transmitted as such" (ibid., 70) by certain socially defined types of transmitters to certain socially defined types of recipients. The structures of the distribution of knowledge (which types transmit which knowledge to whom) differ from society to society.[13] Expressed radically, this means "that social institutions—and social facts in general—are nothing other than the socially distributed, generally shared, collectively and bindingly defined, and—in one way or another—permanently installed knowledge about them or about the action patterns appropriate to them" (Hitzler 1988: 68f; our translation). This pretheoretical primary knowledge about individual institutions and the institutional order in general is not complex. Rather, it is simply structured in easily memorized formulae, expressions, sayings, stylized tales, etc. These can be more easily transmitted by the social types defined as knowers or transmitters—sometimes using physical objects (such as fetishes) and/or symbolic actions (such as rites and rituals) as mnemotechnical aids—and more readily accepted and memorized by the types defined as recipients.

Berger and Luckmann (1966a: 92) use the term legitimation to denote the process whereby institutions are covered with a layer of second-order objectivations and are thereby successfully integrated into an institutional order:

> Legitimation produces new meanings that serve to integrate the meanings already attached to disparate institutional processes. The function of legitimation is to make objectively available and subjectively plausible the "first-order" objectivations that have been institutionalized. While we define legitimation by this function, regardless of the specific motives inspiring any particular legitimating process, it should be added that "integration," in one form or another, is also the typical purpose motivating the legitimators.

The authors (ibid., 94–95) distinguish analytically between four levels of legitimation: First, self-evident knowledge built into the vocabulary: "For example, the transmission of a kinship vocabulary *ipso facto* legitimates the kinship structure." Second, rudimentary theoretical propositions in the form of wise sayings, proverbs, sagas, etc. Third, explicit legitimating theories. For example, a clan may have "an elaborate economic theory of 'cousinhood', its rights, obligations and standard operating procedures." And finally, fourth, symbolic universes of meaning—that is, bodies of theoretical tradition with great integrative and explanatory power—and theoretical universe-maintenance structures, namely mythology, theology, philosophy, and science. The similarities between these four levels of legitimation and Scheler's (1980: 76) typology of *"relatively artificial, or 'learned' world-view forms"* are evident.[14] However, Berger and Luckmann elaborate on their levels of legitimation with reference to the transmission of knowledge, that is, to "meaningful, objectivated channels via which action structures are transmitted. Or, more precisely, [these levels] represent the communicatively transmitted meaning dimension of actions" (Knoblauch 2005: 159; our translation; for a fundamental analysis cf. Luckmann 1986). Theoretical constructions are not the only structures that support symbolic universes. Social organization—in other words increasing division of labor and the "concomitant organization of personnel for the administration of the specialized bodies of knowledge"—are also machineries of universe maintenance (Berger & Luckmann 1966a: 116–17). The authors (ibid., 118–19) give a dramatic account of the manner in which, under pluralistic conditions, resentment on the part of practitioners or laymen toward experts, and rivalry between experts exacerbate social conflict.

No comprehensive description of the social construction of reality would be complete without an analysis of the process by which objectivated social reality is entrenched in consciousness. Section III of *The Social Construction of Reality* (ibid., 129f.) is devoted to this process. In their analysis, Berger and Luckmann draw heavily on Mead and Cooley's insights into processes of socialization and mirroring, in the course of which the self and a personal identity are formed. Hence, they understand internalization as:

> the immediate apprehension or interpretation of an objective event as expressing meaning, that is, as a manifestation of another's subjective processes which thereby becomes subjectively meaningful to myself. (ibid., 129)

The fact that internalization is a *process* is reflected in the authors' description of the transition from "significant other" to "generalized other." On completion of this process, a symmetry is established between objective and subjective reality. However, they stress that this symmetry cannot be complete: "The two realities correspond to each other, but they are not coextensive. . . . No individual internalizes the totality of what is objectivated as reality in his society" (ibid., 133). The gradual nature of internalization is also clearly underlined by the differentiation between primary and secondary socialization. In the latter stage, not only is the world of the generalized other internalized but also institutional or institution-based subworlds (ibid., 138).

Language—or conversation—plays a fundamental role not only in the socialization process but also in the maintenance of subjective reality. As Berger and Luckmann (ibid., 152) argue, "One may view the individual's everyday life in terms of the working away of a conversational apparatus that ongoingly maintains, modifies, and reconstructs his subjective reality." Or, more generally, specific plausibility structures, that is, supportive interchanges with more or less relevant others, form the basis of the maintenance of subjective reality.[15] However, these structures do not guarantee that individuals will be able to cope with crisis situations—especially, but not exclusively, marginal situations such as death—where subjective reality threatens to collapse.

And, finally, Berger and Luckmann analyze the phenomenon of the "transformation" of subjective reality. They use the term "alternation" to denote the extreme case, that is, the near-total exchange of one subjective reality for another, which calls for processes of re-socialization similar to primary socialization (ibid., 156–57). They argue that: "maximal success in socialization is likely to occur in societies with very simple division of labor and minimal distribution of knowledge" (ibid., 164) rather than in modern societies, where different socializing personnel may mediate contradictory versions of objective realities to the individual, or where there may be a discrepancy between primary and secondary socialization (ibid., 167ff.) The connection between internalization and social structure is ultimately revealed by the fact that specific social structures generate specific identity types. This is due, not least, to the fact that the more complex and socially established theories about identity are, the greater their reality-generating or socializing potency (ibid., 178). One example of such a potent theory is psychoanalysis in America (cf. Berger 1965b).

With regard to the concept of knowledge outlined in *The Social Construction of Reality* (1966a), one could view the book as a contribution to what Plessner in his preface to the German-language edition calls the "sociology of the quasi-natural worldview." That would render its interpretation easier—at first. However, it would not do justice to the authors' achievement, because, with their concept of knowledge, they spanned a bridge between micro- and macrosociology. In so doing, they offered American sociology, in particular, a way to overcome the divide between structural functionalism, which had cut itself off from the micro-level, and social psychology—including symbolic interactionism—which was suspicious of the macro-level (cf. Wuthnow et al. 1985: 54). However, the authors' most exceptional achievement is that they identified the field of conflict between the constituting consciousness of the individual actor and socially objectivated constructions of reality, and marked it out for future research (cf. Luckmann 1999; for an overview, cf. Dreher 2007).

5.3 What Is New about the New Sociology of Knowledge?

"If the sociology of knowledge is to be true to its name, it must deal with everything that passes for knowledge in society." This remark, made more or less in passing by Alfred Schutz during a lecture on the sociology of knowledge, so impressed Peter L. Berger that he can still quote it verbatim. It provided the impetus for *The Social Construction of Reality* (1966a), the book that was to lay the foundations of the new sociology of knowledge. In the Introduction, Berger and Luckmann (1966a: 16) acknowledge their indebtedness to their teacher Alfred Schutz, to whom they owed the insight into the necessity to redefine the scope of the sociology of knowledge. They quote Schutz & Natanson (1982: 149), who argued that "typifications of common-sense thinking," rather than ideas and ideologies, are the genuine subject-matter of the sociology of knowledge. These typifications "are themselves integral elements of the concrete socio-cultural *Lebenswelt* within which they prevail as taken for granted and as socially approved" (loc. cit.). Although Berger and Luckmann (1966a: 15) regard the exaggeration of the importance of theoretical thought as a "natural failing of theorizers," they consider it "all the more necessary to correct this intellectualistic misapprehension."

Berger and Luckmann (ibid., 12) follow Werner Stark (1958) when they argue that the task of the sociology of knowledge is not *Ideologiekritik*, that is, "the debunking or uncovering of socially produced distortions." However, in their view, Stark's sociology of knowledge focuses too narrowly on "the sphere of ideas, that is, of theoretical thought" (1966a: 13) and on the problem of truth.

The concept of knowledge on which the authors base their treatise is broad rather than sharply contoured. It does not concern itself with whether knowledge is true, but rather with that which is given the status of knowledge in a particular society, and is thus socially approved as knowledge. In this way, they avoid the distinction between *episteme* and *doxa* inherent in epistemology—a distinction that is untenable from a sociology-of-knowledge perspective. They also avoid the "positivistic conception of knowledge" (Knoblauch 2005: 113) that can be found in Stark's approach and that is inherent—in a much more naive form—in concepts of the "knowledge society" (ibid., 256). Hence, their sociology of knowledge is "an enormous elaboration of Pascal's insight into the social relativity of human notions of truth. Put differently, the sociology of knowledge understands and studies the *constructed* character of what human beings mean by 'reality'" (Berger & Kellner 1981: 59).

Although Peter L. Berger acknowledges that Werner Stark's sociology of knowledge exerted quite a considerable influence on the *Sociological Construction of Reality* (1966a), the two approaches are, nonetheless, incompatible. According to Stark (1991 [1958]: 107), the subject matter of the sociology of knowledge lies in the area between the poles of consciousness and objective reality. Therefore, what Stark (ibid., 108) calls the "categorial layer of the mind" and "the physical apparatus of perception" is excluded from the area of competence of the sociology of knowledge.[16] By contrast, Berger and Luckmann contend that the sociology of knowledge cannot restrict itself to false consciousness or valid knowledge. Rather, it must concern itself with commonsense knowledge—that is, "with everything that passes for 'knowledge' in society" (1966a: 14–15), while bearing in mind that all knowledge is constituted in consciousness.

In the classical sociology of knowledge, "knowledge and structure were analyzed separately, and the focus of the sociological analysis was the correlation between the two" (Kieserling 2010: 435; our translation). In the new sociology of knowledge established by Berger and Luckmann, on the other hand, knowledge and social structure are not considered to be separate spheres that are correlated by virtue of the fact that the individual's location, position, or anchorage in the social structure (social class, generation, political party, etc.) determines thought. Rather, knowledge is deemed to be constitutive of social order and of the entire construction of reality, insofar as it is knowledge that congeals as reality. Hence, knowledge and social structure—like meaning and action—form an indissoluble entity.[17] The new sociology of knowledge takes up the thread spun in Marx's early writings, in which he emphasizes the permanent dialectic between human activity (substructure) and the world produced by that activity (superstructure). This contrasts sharply with later Marxism's politically motivated distinction between—or rather strict counterposing of—substructure and superstructure. In contradistinction to Scheler's moderate sociology of knowledge, and to Mannheim's radical sociology of knowledge, the new sociology of knowledge can be regarded as even more radical because—in contrast to these two correlation-oriented approaches—it breaks new ground by taking an integrative approach to the sociology of knowledge (cf. Knoblauch 2005: 17 and McCarthy 1996: 12).

The decision to exclude questions concerning the existential determination of sociological thought from empirical sociology and to relegate them to the methodology of the social sciences—that is, to the area of competence of philosophy (Berger & Luckmann 1966a: 13)—can be regarded as an inadmissible restriction of the sociology of knowledge. Because sociology concerns itself with social order, it must furnish answers to two fundamental questions: (a) How is social order possible? and (b) How is sociological knowledge possible? According to Kieserling (2010), Berger and Luckmann's sociology of knowledge answers only the first question, while Mannheim's classical sociology of knowledge answers only the second one. At the same time, Kieserling argues that the development of a sociological theory of knowledge—in other words, of a sociology of philosophy or of the history of ideas—is a genuine task of the sociology of knowledge that cannot simply be transferred to philosophy. In his view, therefore, the price Berger and Luckmann have to pay for their decision is that they can concern themselves with everything that passes for knowledge except their own (sociological) knowledge.[18]

However, Berger and Luckmann's decision can also be considered as a step into independence. Tänzler (2006: 318; our translation) argues that:

> The new sociology of knowledge emancipates itself from its inferior position as maid-servant to philosophy, to which it was condemned until Mannheim, and rises to the rank of mistress in its own house—which is quite paradoxical considering that it does so when formulating a theory of knowledge and reality of philosophical relevance.

As Tänzler sees it, Berger and Luckmann forgo the quest for an absolute standpoint and opt for the resolute acceptance of the relativist consequences (ibid., 325). Plessner (1985: 65; our translation) asserts that "Empirical sociology must link this acceptance with the methodologically stipulated restriction to the limits of empirical control." Plessner, too, regards *The Social Construction of Reality* (1966a) as an act of liberation from the sociology of knowledge of the 1920s associated with Scheler and Mannheim. In its effort to protect non-partisan understanding from the accusation of ideological distortion, the sociology of knowledge of Scheler and Mannheim had been "a theory of bad conscience towards Marx," as Plessner notes in his preface to the German-language edition of *The Social Construction of Reality* (Berger & Luckmann 1969: xi).

Berger and Luckmann's insistence that epistemological questions be excluded from the sociology of knowledge is not intended as a retreat from this problem. On the contrary, the new sociology of knowledge, in particular, has paid great attention to the methodology of the social sciences and to self-reflection on the part of the sociology of knowledge. The hermeneutic sociology of knowledge, in which Hans-George Soeffner, in particular, has been an integrative driving force, is devoted to the empirical analysis of the ontological relationship between the individual and the world as he sees it rather than to a critical theory of existential determination.[19] Methodologically speaking, it aims to develop a theory of the understanding of understanding (*Verstehen*) that takes the interpretation of acts and acts of interpretation into account (cf. Soeffner 1989). The epistemological significance of the hermeneutic sociology of knowledge lies "in a 'reform' of social scientific thought in general that begins with a critical analysis of its own practice" (Hitzler et al. 1999: 11; our translation). In this context, not only has the problem of the validity of qualitative social research become the subject of self-reflection on the part of the sociology of knowledge and therefore a "sociology of sociology" (Reichertz 2006: 294) but rather, all sociological findings are assigned the epistemological status of constructions. Hence the conviction that the attitude of methodological skepticism (cf. Berger & Kellner 1981) must not only be assumed with regard to the objectivity of social constructions, but must also be extended to scientific constructions. This is what is meant by a "self-reflective sociology of knowledge." However, as Hitzler (1999: 304; our translation) stresses:

> This does not imply that in every concrete sociological analysis of constructions of reality the constructed nature of these analyses must be also be analyzed, and so on. In other words, it does not imply that every discipline-specific why-question must be followed by a why-question about the why-question, thereby constantly—and vainly—attempting to push the bus one is riding, as Berger and Luckmann (1966a: 13) put it. Rather, it "merely" means that we should follow Soeffner's advice (cf. 1989) and use a "laxative against fundamental considerations"—also, and especially, when our own professional blinkers are what is causing us problems.

Notes

1.   Alexander von Schelting (1934: 84), on the other hand, suggested that the sociology of knowledge be renamed the "sociology of thinking." Werner Stark (1991 [1958]: 123) disagrees. Following Scheler, he argues "that the social, i.e.

the axiological factor is operative in the inception and constitution of a world-view (in our coming-to-know reality) rather than its further elaboration."

2.   Berger appears to have a type of triangulation in mind here. Jo Reichertz (2006: 294–95; our translation) points out that Berger and Luckmann understand epistemology "mainly as the interpretation of society *by* scientists," whereas Soeffner and later protagonists of the sociology of knowledge have focused on "scientists' *own* self-observation and self-interpretation."

3.   Wuthnow et al. (1984: 33) also point out that Berger's concept of objectivity is not Popperian.

4.   "If it is to be a science of reality—what Max Weber called the 'sociology of reality'—sociology must always also be sociology of knowledge—a theory of social knowing and not-knowing. It combines self-reflection with reflection about social knowledge and, in so doing, inevitably encounters the limits of knowledge and the limitations of sociological perception" (Tänzler, Knoblauch & Soeffner 2006: 7; our translation).

5.   In view of the misunderstandings that the concept of construction has caused among readers and critics of the book, Berger now tends to think that the term "definition" or "interpretation" might have been a better choice because what he and Luckmann had proposed was that "all reality is subject to socially derived interpretations" and not that "there is nothing here but our constructions" (Berger & Zijderveld 2009: 66).

6.   "In everyday life, the type [is] a situational interpretation for action that assigns neutral operations to familiar meaning contexts, thereby transforming them into specific sequences—that is, into sequences imbued with a specific meaning. This occurs without the necessity of special activities of consciousness—the assignment takes place automatically" (Srubar 1979: 45; our translation). However, that does not mean that it is an arbitrary process. Although typification processes take place without our active input, they are regulated by the relevances that have formed in previous activities of consciousness (cf. Knoblauch 2005: 144).

7.   Luckmann (1999: 17) attributes this thought to Giambattista Vico, whose thesis "verum ipsum factum" ("truth itself is constructed") is inherently social-constructionist.

8.   By "objectivation" Berger and Luckmann (1966a: 60) understand: "The process by which the externalized products of human activity attain the character of objectivity." The term is derived from the Hegelian/Marxian *Versachlichung* (ibid.,197, Note 28) and is explicitly *not* related to "what Marx called a reification (*Verdinglichung*), that is, an undialectical distortion of social reality" (ibid.,198, Note 29; cf. also Note 58: 200). In the authors' view, then contemporary American sociology, and especially structural functionalism, contributed to further obscuring the fact that "the man on the street" does not realize that institutional order originates in human activity (cf. also Berger & Pullberg 1965e).

9.   "Knowledge transforms subjective meaning into social facts, and knowledge transforms social facts into subjective meaning" (Hitzler 1988: 65; our translation).

10. In his detailed account of the social-constructivist line of argument Knoblauch (2005: 157) begins by noting "that institutionalization builds on the analysis of the interaction."

11. "Institutions are embodied in individual experience by means of roles. . . . By playing roles, the individual participates in a social world. By internalizing these roles, the same world becomes subjectively real to him" (Berger & Luckmann 1966a: 74). Each role has its own socially defined stock of knowledge. Therefore, roles impart special extracts from the social stock of knowledge (cf. Pfadenhauer 1998).

12. In this sense, Kieserling (2010: 434) is correct in describing the thematic history of the sociology of knowledge as movement from "theoretical to practical knowledge."

13. These historically specific structures of the distribution of social knowledge are termed the "social stock of knowledge." The complementary term is the "subjective stock of knowledge" (cf. Schutz & Luckmann 1973). The subjective stock of knowledge comprises both experiential—first-hand—knowledge and knowledge elements that are not constituted by the individual's own consciousness but rather transmitted by others, i.e. second-hand knowledge (Hitzler 1988: 62; cf. Schutz & Luckmann 1973). Gurwitsch (1971: xxiii; our translation) puts it even more explicitly: "Everything that I have acquired personally, that I have appropriated, presupposes a socially derived 'available stock of knowledge,' insofar as these acquired elements must be integrated into that socially derived framework and must find their place there. Personally acquired [knowledge] is never isolated."

14. Scheler (1980: 76) enumerates the types of artificial world-view forms by their degree of artificiality, starting with the least-artificial type: "1. *myth and legend*; . . . 2. the knowledge implicit in everyday *natural language*; . . . 3. the *religious knowledge* . . . from pious, emotive and vague intuition up to the fixated dogmas of a priestly church; 4. the basic forms of *mystical knowledge*; 5. *philosophic-metaphysical knowledge*; 6. the *positive knowledge* of mathematics and of the natural sciences and the humanities; and 7. *technological knowledge*." On Scheler's sociology of knowledge as "an a priori, i.e. non-empirical theory of contents of human consciousness in interdependence with organizational forms that 'reflect' these elements of consciousness," compare Honer (1999: 59–60; our translation).

15. The similarity between plausibility structures and what Goffman (1971: 62) terms "supportive interchanges" is striking. Luckmann (2007a: 90; our translation) refers to the "credibility structure that supports the worldview." And Berger and Kellner (1981: 60) note that "The social context for any set of norms or alleged bodies of 'knowledge' is the plausibility structure."

16. In his theory for the sociology of knowledge, Stark takes as his starting point the social *a priori* or the "axiological system," which, in his view, is co-extensive with the society's system of values. It enables "those searching for socio-historical truths" to distinguish between the important and the unimportant. Hence, Stark does not completely ignore consciousness. However, he is interested only in the social determination of consciousness and of the contents of consciousness. Like Scheler, Stark is interested in the value-determination (*Wertegebundenheit*) of knowledge rather than its existential determination (*Seinsgebundenheit*). In this way, he integrates Weber's theory of elective affinity as "gradual convergence between substructure and superstructure" (Eisermann 1960: vii) into the functionalist notion of society: "On the one hand, institutions form themselves and achieve

comparative fixity, on the other hand modal ideas; and both poles thus produced—ideas and institutions—are determined by, and characteristic of, the parent reality, which has brought them forth" (1991 [1958]: 244).

17. That is the reason why Kieserling (2010: 436) criticizes this concept of knowledge as "indifferent."

18. Kieserling derives his prognosis that the sociology of sociological knowledge will remain in a bad way from a sociology-of-knowledge argument. He asserts that, because contemporary sociologists of knowledge no longer have a solid basic education in philosophy, they are no longer inclined to concern themselves with philosophical questions.

19. Compare also Tänzler (2006). Berger and Luckmann's interest in religion meant that the social world structured by meaning became the focus of attention as a "world of culture." As Berger (1967: 6–7) notes: "Culture consists of the totality of man's products. . . . Society is that aspect of the [non-material, MP] culture that structures man's ongoing relations with his fellow-men."

Identity as a Problem in the Sociology of Knowledge

by Peter L. Berger

It is through the work of George Herbert Mead and the Meadian tradition of the "symbolic-interactionist" school that a theoretically viable social psychology has been founded. Indeed, it may be maintained that in this achievement lies the most important *theoretical* contribution made to the social sciences in America. The perspectives of the Meadian tradition have become established within American sociology far beyond the school that explicitly seeks to represent them. Just as it was sociologists who "discovered" Mead at the University of Chicago and diffused his ideas beyond the latter's confines, so the social psychology constituted on this foundation continues to be the one to which sociologists gravitate most naturally in their theoretical assumptions, a "sociologist's psychology," despite the later competition from psychoanalysis and learning theory.[1] By contrast, the sociology of knowledge has remained marginal to the discipline in this country, still regarded widely as an unassimilated European import of interest only to a few colleagues with a slightly eccentric penchant for the history of ideas.[2] This marginality of the sociology of knowledge is not difficult to explain in terms of the historical development of sociological theory in this country. All the same, it is rather remarkable that the theoretical affinity between the sociology of knowledge and social psychology in the Meadian tradition has not been widely recognized. One might argue that there has been an implicit recognition in the linkage of social psychology, by way of role theory and reference group theory, with the psychology of cognitive processes, particularly in the work of Robert Merton, Muzafer Sherif and Tamotsu Shibutani.[3] In the case of Merton, however, the discussion of the cognitive implications of social-psychological processes occurs in a curious segregation from the treatment of the sociology of knowledge, while in the cases of Sherif and Shibutani there appears to be no conscious connection with the sociology of knowledge at all.

Understandable historically, this segregation is theoretically deplorable. Social psychology has been able to show how the subjective reality of individual consciousness is socially constructed. The sociology of knowledge, as Alfred Schutz has indicated, may be understood as the sociological critique of consciousness, concerning itself with the social construction of reality in general.[4] Such a critique entails the analysis of both "objective reality" (that is, "knowledge" about the world, as objectivated and taken for granted in society) and its subjective correlates (that is, the modes in which this objectivated world is subjectively plausible or "real" to the individual). If these shorthand descriptions of the two sub-disciplines are allowed, then integration between them is not an exotic miscegenation but a bringing together of two partners by the inner logic of their natures. Obviously this paper cannot develop the details of such a project of theoretical integration, but it may indicate some general directions and implications.

Social psychology has brought about the recognition that the sphere of psychological phenomena is continuously permeated by social forces, and more than that, is decisively shaped by the latter. "Socialization" means not only that the self-consciousness of the individual is constituted in a specific form by society (which Mead called the "social genesis of the self"), but that psychological reality is in an ongoing dialectical relationship with social structure. Psychological reality refers here, *not* to scientific or philosophical propositions *about* psychological phenomena, but to the manner in which the individual apprehends himself, his processes of consciousness and his relations with others. Whatever its anthropological-biological roots, psychological reality arises in the individual's biography in the course of social processes and is only maintained (that is, maintained in consciousness *as* "reality") by virtue of social processes. Socialization not only ensures that the individual is "real" to himself in a certain way, but that he will ongoingly respond to his experience of the world with the cognitive and emotive patterns appropriate to this "reality." For example, successful socialization shapes a self that apprehends itself exclusively and in a taken-for-granted way in terms of one or the other of two socially defined sexes, that "knows" this self-apprehension to be the only "real" one, and rejects as "unreal" any contrary modes of apprehension or emotionality. Self and society are inextricably interwoven entities.

Their relationship is dialectical because the self, once formed, may act back in its turn upon the society that shaped it (a dialectic that Mead expressed in his formulation of the "I" and the "me"). The self exists by virtue of society, but society is only possible as many selves continue to apprehend themselves and each other with reference to it.[5]

Every society contains a repertoire of identities that is part of the "objective knowledge" of its members. It is "known" as a matter "of course" that there are men and women, that they have such-and-such psychological traits and that they will have such-and-such psychological reactions in typical circumstances. As the individual is socialized, these identities are "internalized." They are then not only taken for granted as constituents of an objective reality "out there" but as inevitable structures of the individual's own consciousness. The objective reality, as defined by society, is subjectively appropriated. In other words, socialization brings about symmetry between objective and subjective reality, objective and subjective identity. The degree of this symmetry provides the criterion of the successfulness of socialization. The psychological reality of the successfully socialized individual thus *verifies* subjectively what his society has objectively defined as real. He is then no longer required to turn outside himself for "knowledge" concerning the nature proper of men and women. He can obtain that result by simple introspection. He "knows who he is." He feels accordingly. He can conduct himself "spontaneously," because the firmly internalized cognitive and emotive structures make it unnecessary or even impossible for him to reflect upon alternative possibilities of conduct.[6]

This dialectic between social structure and psychological reality may be called the fundamental proposition of any social psychology in the Meadian tradition. Society not only defines but creates psychological reality. The individual *realizes* himself in society—that is, he recognizes his identity in socially defined terms and these definitions *become reality* as he lives in society. This fundamentally Meadian dialectic makes intelligible the social-psychological scope of W. I. Thomas' concept of the "definition of the situation" as well as of Merton's of the "self-fulfilling prophecy."[7]

The sociology of knowledge is concerned with a related but broader dialectic—that between social structure and the "worlds" in which individuals live, that is, the comprehensive organizations of reality within which individual experience can be meaningfully interpreted.[8] Every society is a world-building enterprise. Out of the near-infinite

117

variety of individual symbolizations of experience society constructs a universe of discourse that comprehends and objectivates them. Individual experience can then be understood as taking place in an intelligible world that is inhabited also by others and about which it is possible to communicate with others. Individual meanings are objectivated so that they are accessible to everyone who coinhabits the world in question. Indeed, this world is apprehended as "objective reality," that is, as reality that is shared with others and that exists irrespective of the individual's own preferences in the matter. The socially available definitions of such a world are thus taken to be "knowledge" about it and are continuously verified for the individual by social situations in which this "knowledge" is taken for granted. The socially constructed world becomes the world *tout court*—the only real world, typically the only world that one can seriously conceive of. The individual is thus freed of the necessity of reflecting anew about the meaning of each step in his unfolding experience. He can simply refer to "common sense" for such interpretation, at least for the great bulk of his biographical experience.[9]

Language is both the foundation and the instrumentality of the social construction of reality.[10] Language focalizes, patterns and objectivates individual experience. Language is the principal means by which an individual is socialized to become an inhabitant of a world shared with others and also provides the means by which, in conversation with these others, the common world continues to be plausible to him.[11] On this linguistic base is erected the edifice of interpretative schemes, cognitive and moral norms, value systems and, finally, theoretically articulated "world-views" which, in their totality, form the world of "collective representations" (as the Durkheimian school put it) of any given society.[12] Society *orders* experience. Only in a world of social order can there develop a "collective consciousness" which permits the individual to have a subjectively meaningful life and protects him from the devastating effects of *anomie,* that is, from a condition in which the individual is deprived of the social ordering processes and thus deprived of meaning itself. It is useful to remind oneself of the linguistic base of all social order whenever one theorizes about the latter, because language makes particularly clear just what is meant by the social construction of an objectively real world. Language is undeniably a social invention and a linguistic system cannot be credited with an ontological status apart from the society that invented it. Nevertheless, the individual learns his language (especially, of course, his native language) as an objective reality.[13] He cannot change it at will. He must conform to its coercive power. Typically, he is unable to conceive of either the world or of himself except through the conceptual modalities which it provides. But this facticity, externality and coerciveness of language (the very traits that constitute the Durkheimian *choseïté*, or thing-like character, of social phenomena) extends to all the objectivations of society. The subjective consequence is that the individual "finds himself" (that is, apprehends himself as placed, willy-nilly) in the social world as much as in nature.

It is important to stress that the social construction of reality takes place on both the pre-theoretical and the theoretical levels of consciousness, and that, therefore, the sociology of knowledge must concern itself with both. Probably because of the German intellectual situation in which the sociology of knowledge was first developed, it has hitherto interested itself predominantly in the theoretical side of the phenomenon—the problem of the relationship of society and "ideas."[14] This is certainly an important problem. But only very few people are worried over "ideas," while everyone lives in some sort of a world. There is thus a sociological dimension to the human activity of worldbuilding in its totality, not only in that segment of it in which intellectuals manufacture theories, systems of thought, and *Weltanschauungen*. Thus, in the matter under discussion here, the sociology of knowledge has an interest not only in various theories *about* psychological phenomena (what one may call a sociology of psychology) but in these phenomena themselves (what one may then, perhaps impertinently, call a sociological psychology).

The relationship between a society and its world is a dialectic one because, once more, it cannot be adequately understood in terms of a one-sided causation.[15] The world, though socially constructed, is not a mere passive reflection of the social structures within which it arose. In becoming "objective reality" for its inhabitants it attains not only a certain autonomy with respect to the "underlying" society but even the power to act back upon the latter. Men invent a language and then find that its logic imposes itself upon them. And men concoct theories, even theories that may start out as nothing but blatant explications of social interests, and then discover that these theories themselves become agencies of social change. It may be seen, then, that there is a theoretically significant similarity between the dialectics of social psychology and of the sociology of knowledge, the dialectic through which society generates psychological reality and the dialectic through

119

which it engages in world-building. Both dialectics concern the relationship between objective and subjective realities, or more precisely, between socially objectivated reality and its subjective appropriation. In both instances, the individual internalizes facticities that appear to him as given outside himself and, having internalized them to become given contents of his own consciousness, externalizes them again as he continues to live and act in society.[16]

These considerations, especially in the compressed form in which they have had to be presented here, may at first seem to be excessively abstract. Yet, if one asks about the combined significance of these root perspectives of social psychology and the sociology of knowledge for the sociological understanding of identity, one may answer in a rather simple statement: *Identity, with its appropriate attachments of psychological reality, is always identity within a specific, socially constructed world.* Or, as seen from the viewpoint of the individual: *One identifies oneself as one is identified by others, by being located in a common world.*

Socialization is only possible if, as Mead put it, the individual "takes the attitude" of others, that is, relates to himself as others have first related to him. This process, of course, extends to the establishment of identity itself, so that one may formulate that social identification both precedes and produces self-identification. Now, it is possible that the Meadian process of attitude- and role-taking occurs between individuals who do not share a common world—for instance, between Columbus and the very first American Indians he met in 1492. Even they, however, soon identified each other within a world which they inhabited together, or more accurately, they together established such a world as they dealt with each other. Socializing each other in terms of this world, they could then take on the attitudes and roles appropriate within it. Columbus and his Spaniards, being (like parents in this respect) the stronger party, had the edge in this game of "naming"—the others had to identify themselves in the Spaniards' terms, namely as *Indios,* while the Spaniards were probably little tempted to identify themselves with the mythological creatures as which they in turn were first identified by the others. In other words, the American Indian identified himself by locating himself in the Spaniard's world, though, to be sure, that world was itself modified as he became its co-inhabitant. In the more normal cases of socialization, occurring between individuals who already co-inhabit the same world, it is even easier to see how identification entails location in that world from the beginning. The parents give their child a name and then deal with him in terms appropriate to this identification. The literal act of "naming," of course, is already location in this sense (its exactitude depending upon the culture" John Smith" being less satisfactory as an "address" than "Ivan Ivanovitch, Village-Idiot," and so forth). However, as the full implications of the name and its location unfold in the course of socialization, the child appropriates the world in which he is thus located in the same process in which he appropriates his identity—a moral universe as he identifies himself as a "good baby," a sexual universe as a "little boy," a class universe as a "little gentleman"—and so on. One may expand the Meadian phrase, then, by saying that the individual takes the world of others as he takes their attitudes and roles. Each role implies a world. The self is always located in a world. The *same* process of socialization generates the self and internalizes the world to which this self belongs.

The same reasoning applies to psychological reality in general. Just as any particular psychological reality is attached to a socially defined identity, so it is located in a socially constructed world. As the individual identifies and locates himself in the world of his society, he finds himself the possessor of a pre-defined assemblage of psychological processes, both "conscious" and "unconscious" ones, and even some with somatic effects. The "good baby" feels guilty after a temper tantrum, the "little boy" channels his erotic fantasies towards little girls, the "little gentleman" experiences revulsion when someone engages in public nose-picking—and this revulsion may, under the proper conditions, affect his stomach to the point of vomitation. Every socially constructed world thus contains a repertoire of identities and a corresponding psychological system. The social definition of identity takes place as part of an overarching definition of reality. The internalization of the world, as it occurs in socialization, imposes upon consciousness a psychological as well as a cognitive structure, and (to a degree which has as yet not been adequately clarified scientifically) even extends into the area of physiological processes.[17] Pascal indicated the root problem of the sociology of knowledge when he observed that what is truth on one side of the Pyrénées is error on the other. The same observation applies to the good conscience and the bad (including the "unconscious" manifestations of the latter), to the libidinously interesting and the libidinously indifferent, as well as to what upsets and what relaxes the gastric juices. And, of course, a French identity differs appreciably from a Spanish one.[18]

A third dialectic may be analyzed if one now turns to the theoretical level of consciousness—that between psychological reality and psychological models. Men not only experience themselves. They also explain themselves. While these explanations differ in their degrees of sophistication, it would be difficult to conceive of a society without some theoretical explication of the psychological nature of man. Whether such explication takes the form of proverbial wisdom, mythology, metaphysics or scientific generalization is, of course, a different question. What all these forms have in common is that they systematize the experience of psychological reality on a certain level of abstraction. They constitute psychological models, by means of which individual psychological processes can be compared, typified and thus "prepared for treatment." For example, individuals in a society may have all kinds of visionary experiences. Both the individuals themselves and those with whom they live are faced with the question of what these experiences signify. A psychological model that "explains" such occurrences allows them to compare any particular experience with the several species codified in the model. The experience may then be classified in terms of this typology—as a case of demon possession, say, or as a mark of sacred status, or as merely crazy in a profane mode. This application of the psychological model (the "diagnosis") then permits a decision on what to do about the occurrence (the "therapy"—to exorcise the individual, to beatify him, or possibly to award him the role of buffoon and of menace to disobedient children. In other words, the psychological model locates individual experience and conduct within a comprehensive theoretical system.[19]

It goes without saying that each psychological model is embedded in a more general theoretical formulation of reality. The model is part of the society's general "knowledge about the world," raised to the level of theoretical thought. Thus a psychological model that contains a typology of possession belongs to a religious conception of the world as such and a psychological theory of "mental illness," as understood by contemporary psychiatry, is located in a much wider "scientific" conception of the world and of man's place in it. *Psychological "knowledge" is always part of a general "knowledge about the world"*—in this proposition lies the foundation of what, a little earlier, was called the sociology of psychology. The import of this proposition can be conveyed by referring to the psychiatric concept of "reality orientation." A psychiatrist may decide that a certain individual is not adequately "oriented to reality" and, therefore, "mentally ill." The sociologist may then accept this description, but must immediately ask—*"which reality?"* Just as cultural anthropology has been able to demonstrate that the manifestations of the Freudian "pleasure principle" vary from one society to another, so the sociology of knowledge must insist an a similar socio-cultural relativization of the Freudian "reality principle."[20]

This sociological perspective has far-reaching implications for the analysis of psychological theories. As has been indicated, every socially constructed world contains a psychological model. If this model is to retain its plausibility, it must have some empirical relationship to the psychological reality objectivated in the society. A demonological model is "unreal" in contemporary society. The psychoanalytic one is not. It is important to stress once again the matter of empirical verification. Just as the individual can verify his socially assigned identity by introspection, so the psychological theoretician can verify his model by "empirical research." If the model corresponds to the psychological reality as socially defined and produced, it will quite naturally be verified by empirical investigation of this reality. This is not quite the same as saying that psychology is self-verifying. It rather says that the data discovered by a particular psychology belong to the same socially constructed world that has also produced that psychology.

Once more, the relationship between psychological reality and psychological model is a dialectic one. The psychological reality produces the psychological model, insofar as the model is an empirically verifiable representation of the reality. Once formed, however, the psychological model can act back upon the psychological reality. The model has *realizing* potency, that is, it can create psychological reality as a "self-fulfilling prophecy." In a society in which demonology is socially established, cases of demon possession will empirically multiply. A society in which psychoanalysis is institutionalized as "science" will become populated by people who, in fact, evince the processes that have been theoretically attributed to them. It should be clear that this self-fulfilling character of psychological models is grounded in the same dialectic of socialization that Mead first formulated with incisive clarity and which can be summarized by saying that men become that as which they are addressed.

The purpose of these brief considerations has been to indicate what theoretical gains might be expected from an integration of the approaches of social psychology in the Meadian tradition and the sociology of knowledge. This is obviously not the place to discuss the methodological issues or the numerous possibilities of empirical exploration arising from such integration.[21] Suffice it to say, in conclusion, that the theoretical viewpoint expressed here implies a serious reconsideration of the relationship between the two disciplines of sociology and psychology. This relationship has been characterized, at least in this country, by a theoretically unjustified timidity an the side of the sociologists and by a spirit of oecumenical tolerance that may have beneficial consequences for inter-departmental amity, but which has not always been conducive to clear sociological thinking.

Notes

1. On the "diffusion" of Meadian social psychology among American sociologists, cf. Anselm STRAUSS (ed.), George Herbert Mead on Social Psychology (Chicago, University of Chicago Press, 1964), pp. vii sqq. For a critique of this Meadian "establishment," from a psychoanalytically oriented viewpoint, cf. Dennis WRONG, "The Over-Socialized Conception of Man in Modern Sociology," Psychoanalysis and the Psychoanalytic Review, XXXIX (1962), pp. 53 sqq.

2. Among American sociologists, the sociology of knowledge has remained rather narrowly associated with its conception by Karl Mannheim, who served as its principal "translator" from the context of German Geisteswissenschaft to that of English-speaking social science. The writings of Max Scheler on Wissenssoziologie (the term was coined by him) remain untranslated today. American sociologists have also, in the main, remained unaffected by the development of the sociology of knowledge in the work of Alfred Schütz, not to mention recent contributions in the positivistic tradition (mainly by sociologists writing in German) and by Marxists (mainly in France). For the Mannheim-oriented reception of the sociology of knowledge in America, cf. Robert MERTON, Social Theory and Social Structure (Glencoe, Ill., Free Press, 1957), pp. 439 sqq., and Talcott PARSONS, "An Approach to the Sociology of Knowledge," Transactions of the Fourth World Congress of Sociology (Louvain, International Sociological Association, 1959). For a conception of the sub-discipline more in the line of Scheler than of Mannheim (and with which the present writer would not associate himself fully, either), cf. Werner STARK, The Sociology of Knowledge (Glencoe, Ill., Free Press, 1958).

3. Cf. MERTON, OP. Cit. pp. 225 sqq.; Muzafer SHERIF and Carolyn SHERIF, An Outline of Social Psychology (New York, Harper, 1956); Tamotsu SHIBUTANI, "Reference Groups and Social Control," in Arnold ROSE (ed.), Human Behavior and Social Processes (Boston, Houghton Mifflin, 1962), pp. 128 sqq.

4. This understanding of the scope of the sociology of knowledge, a much broader one than that of the Mannheim-oriented approach, has been strongly influenced by the work of Alfred Schütz. Cf. Alfred SCHÜTZ, Der sinnhafte Aufbau der sozialen Welt (Vienna, Springer, 1960); The Problem of Social Reality (The Hague, Nijhoff, 1962); Studies in Social Theory (The Hague, Nijhoff, 1964).

124

5.   This dialectic between self and society can also be formulated in Marxian terms. *Cf.*, for example, Joseph GABEL, *La fausse conscience* (Paris, Éditions de Minuit, 1962), and Jean-Paul SARTRE, *Search for a Method* (New York, Knopf, 1963). For an attempt at integrating certain Marxian categories within a non-Marxian sociology of knowledge, *cf.* Peter BERGER and Stanley PULLBERG, "Reification and the Sociological Critique of Consciousness," *History and Theory*, IV (1965).

6.   On the social structuring of conduct, cf. Arnold GEHLEN, Urmensch und Spätkultur (Bonn, Athenaeum, 1956), where Gehlen proposes a biologically grounded theory of social institutions. On this very suggestive theory, which to date has remained practically unknown to American sociologists, also cf. Arnold GEHLEN, Anthropologische Forschung (Hamburg, Rowohlt, 1961), and Studien zur Anthropologie und Soziologie (Neuwied/Rhein Luchterhand, 1963).

7.   Thomas well-known dictum on the "real consequences" of social definition was presumably intended, and has been generally understood as intending, to say that once a "reality" has been defined, people will act as if it were indeed so. To this important proposition must be added an understanding of the realizing (that is, reality-producing) potency of social definition. This social-psychological import of Thomas' "basic theorem" was developed by Merton, op. cit. pp. 421 sqq. The sociology of knowledge, as this paper tries to indicate, would extend this notion of the social construction of "reality" even further.

8.   Cf. SCHUTZ, Problem of Social Reality, pp. 207 sqq.

9.   Cf. ibid. pp. 3 sqq.

10.   Cf. ibid. pp. 287 sqq. Also, cf. Ernst CASSIRER, An Essay on Man (New Haven, Yale University Press, 1962), pp. 109 sqq. The problem of language and "reality," neglected by American sociologists, has been extensively discussed in American cultural anthropology, vide the influence of Edward Sapir and the controversy over the so-called "Whorf hypothesis." It has been a central problem for sociologists and cultural anthropologists in France ever since the Durkheim school. Cf. Claude LÉVI-STRAUSS, La pensée sauvage (Paris, Plon, 1962).

11.   On the maintenance of "reality" by means of the "conversational apparatus," *cf.* Peter BERGER and Hansfried KELLNER, "Le mariage et la construction de la realité," *Diogène*, XLVI (1964), pp. 3 sqq.

12.   One may say that the Durkheimian theory of "collective consciousness" is the positive side of the theory of *anomie*. The *locus classicus* of this is, of course, Durkheim's *Elementary Forms of the Religious Life*. For important developments of this (all of great relevance for the sociology of knowledge), *cf.* Marcel GRANET, *La pensée chinoise* (Paris, Albin Michel, 1950); Maurice HALBWACHS, *Les cadres sociaux de la mémoire* (Paris, P.U.F., 1952); Marcel MAUSS, *Sociologie et anthropologie* (Paris, P.U.F., 1960).

13.   The fullest evidence on the "objectivity" of the child's language learning is to be found in the work of Jean Piaget.

14.   The fixation of the sociology of knowledge on the theoretical level of consciousness is well expressed in the subtitle of the previously cited work by Stark—"An Essay in Aid of a Deeper Understanding of the History of Ideas." The present writer would consider Schutz's work as essential

for arriving at a broader conception of the sub-discipline. For a broader approach based on Marxian presuppositions, *cf.* Henri LEFEBVRE, *Critique de la vie quotidienne* (Paris, L'Arche, 1958–1961). For a discussion of the possibility of using Pareto for a critique of pre-theoretical consciousness in society, *cf.* Brigitte BERGER, *Vilfredo Pareto's Sociology as a Contribution to the Sociology of Knowledge* (Unpublished doctoral dissertation—Graduate Faculty, New School for Social Research, 1964).

15. This problem is, of course, dealt with by Marx in his well-known conception of sub- and super-structure. The present writer would argue that, at least in Marx's early writings (as in the *Economic and Philosophic Manuscripts of 1844)*, the relationship between the two is clearly a dialectic one. In later Marxism, the dialectic is lost in a mechanistic understanding of sub- and super-structure in which the latter becomes a mere epiphenomenon (Lenin—a "reflection") of the former. On this "reification" of Marxism in Communist ideology (perhaps one of the great ironies in the history of ideas), *cf.*, for example, Joseph GABEL, *Formen der Entfremdung* (Frankfurt, Fischer, 1964), pp. 53 sqq. Probably the most important work, within the Marxian tradition, which has tried to recapture the original dialectic in dealing with this problem is Georg LUKÁCS' *Geschichte und Klassenbewußtsein* (1923), now virtually unobtainable in German, but available in an excellent French translation—*Histoire et conscience de classe* (Paris, Éditions de Minuit, 1960).

16. The overarching dialectic of sociation indicated here can be analysed in terms of three "moments"—externalization, objectivation and internalization. The dialectic is lost whenever one of these "moments" is excluded from social theory. *Cf.* BERGER and PULLBERG, *loc. cit.*

17. For indications of the intriguing possibilities of such a "socio-somatics," *cf.* Georg Simmel's discussion of the "sociology of the senses," in his *Soziologie* (Berlin, Duncker & Humblot, 1958), pp. 483 sqq. Also, *cf.* Mauss' essay on the "techniques of the body," in his *op. cit.* pp. 365 sqq.

18. It is not intended here to propose a "sociologistic" view of reality as *nothing but* a social construction. Within the sociology of knowledge, however, it is possible to bracket the final epistemological questions.

19. On the sociology-of-knowledge implications of diagnostic typologies, cf. Eliot FREIDSON, The Sociology of Medicine (Oxford, Blackwell, 1963), pp. 124 sqq.

20. For a critique of the contemporary concept of "mental illness," coming from within psychiatry itself, cf. Thomas SZASZ, The Myth of Mental Illness (New York, Hosber-Harper, 1961).

21. Cf. Peter L. BERGER and Thomas LUCKMANN, *The Social Construction of Reality* (Garden City, Doubleday, 1966).

6

Reception and Impact of the New Sociology of Knowledge

This concluding chapter is devoted to a brief analysis of the reception and impact of Peter L. Berger's work, in particular his sociology of knowledge. I shall be focusing only on the reception of his best-known works, and sharing some impressions gleaned from my encounters with Berger over the last five years.

Berger has produced four bestsellers in his time, all of which were written in the 1960s, and all of which have been translated into many foreign languages: *Invitation to Sociology* (1963a), *The Social Construction of Reality* (Berger & Luckmann 1966a), *The Sacred Canopy* (1967), and *Rumor of Angels* (1969a). He himself attributes their success to the fact that, at the time of publication, their content was very much in tune with the prevailing *zeitgeist*. This was particularly striking in the case of *The Social Construction of Reality* (1966a), whose publication coincided with the height of the left-wing protest movement. The book was carried along by the wave of revolutionary enthusiasm that was spreading to broad sections of the population at the time. Berger recalls that this was really brought home to him one day in 1968 when his secretary informed him with a look of trepidation that "two bearded, possibly dangerous men" wanted to see him. When he asked them in, he noticed that one of them was armed—with the Spanish-language edition of *The Social Construction of Reality*. The man announced that he and his companion were revolutionaries from a country in Latin America, and said, "You write about the construction of society. We want to *re*construct society. Our leader thinks that you might give us advice for our revolutionary project." Berger explained that the book was a theoretical exercise and that he had no useful advice to give: "They were clearly disappointed and soon left, to my (not to mention my secretary's) relief" (2011: 96).

The reception of *The Social Construction of Reality* focused more on its theory-of-society orientation—it was perceived as a blueprint for social constructivism—than on its social theory orientation, that is, the authors' reformulation of the sociology of knowledge. In other words, readers tended to focus on action rather than knowledge. What was obviously overlooked was the fact that by "construction" the authors did not mean the decision of a small group—not to mention an individual—to change reality or social conditions, but rather the emergence of reality "in the course of long-term human activities over generations" (Luckmann 1999: 18; our translation). Although the misunderstanding was probably caused, in part, by the title of the book,[1] the main reason was the *zeitgeist* that prevailed at the time.

The one-sided reception of *The Social Construction of Reality* (1966a) as a social theory, and the failure to recognize its sociology-of-knowledge implications, was undoubtedly due mainly to the fact that it was read superficially. However, the interpretation was also encouraged by the argument structure of the work. Emphasis was placed on the externalization aspect of the dialectical interplay between externalization, objectivation, and internalization. This was intended as a counterbalance to the overemphasis that Berger had placed on internalization—in the Durkheimian sense of the programming of the individual by society—in *Invitation to Sociology* (1963a). And finally, the one-sided interpretation was due also to the fact that, in subsequent comments, Berger—and, even more so, Luckmann—gave the impression that the description, and the subtitling, of the book as "a treatise in the sociology of knowledge" was a (marketing) ploy. In his preface to the German-language edition (1969: x–xi), Helmuth Plessner observes that, while many German sociologists would be irritated by the word "construction" in the title, they would be appeased by the subtitle, because "the sociology of knowledge is an old favorite of German readers." Berger cautiously admits that their confrontation with the sociology of knowledge had covertly yielded a theory of society. And in his laudatory speech on the occasion of the award of the Paul Watzlawick Ring of Honor to Berger in Vienna in 2008, Luckmann stated that *The Social Construction of Reality* was an "alternative to the structural functionalism that dominated sociology at the time, disguised as a theory for the sociology of knowledge" (our translation).

Reflecting on *The Social Construction of Reality* in his career memoir *Adventures of an Accidental Sociologist* (2011: 89), Berger notes that:

> this book was successful far beyond anything we could have imagined when our clique began. It has been described as a "minor classic," a phrase that combines a congratulatory noun with an adjectival putdown. In any case, the book has engendered a whole literature of commentary, both positive and negative. Its influence has gone far beyond sociology.

The Homeless Mind (Berger et al. 1973a) met with a fate similar to that of *The Social Construction of Reality* as far as the failure to recognize its sociology-of-knowledge perspective was concerned. Although it is a genuine contribution to the new sociology of knowledge, highlighting as it does the relationship between the subjective and the social stock of knowledge in modern consciousness, the book was read more as a contribution to the diagnosis of psychological homelessness resulting from modernity. And yet, it offers a large number of fundamental concepts that were to prove useful to phenomenologically orientated, sociology-of-knowledge empiricism. Moreover, it helped to give the new sociology of knowledge clearer contours by marking its boundaries—not only vis-à-vis the field of sociology as a whole but also in relation to epistemology. The work reveals, on the one hand, that the problem of the sociology of knowledge can be defined in general terms as the relationship between structures of consciousness and institutional structures. Although this subject matter also includes philosophical questions (about truth and validity), the sociology of knowledge still remains part of sociology as an empirical discipline. On the other hand, it shows that the sociology of knowledge and sociology are not identical. Put differently, the sociology of knowledge reaches its boundaries when it comes, for example, to the study of institutional dynamics—or, more generally, to the unintended consequences of social action.

Despite the fact that *Invitation to Sociology* (1963a) was "out of step with the *Geist* of early sixties sociology" (Berger 2011: 75), the book soon became a bestseller and has remained so ever since. In *Adventures of an Accidental Sociologist* (2011: 75), Berger notes:

> The American Anchor Books edition reached its one million mark in 1981; I have no idea how many copies it has sold by now. To date there have been twenty-one translations into foreign languages—not

just into the obvious major ones but, among others, into Basque, Lithuanian, and Bahasa Indonesia. I keep running into people who tell me that this book induced them to become sociologists. This is often said in an accusatory tone, because they discovered that what most sociologists do today has little to do with the picture of the discipline conveyed by the book.

The success of *Invitation to Sociology* (1963a) is probably due not least to the fact that it is an introductory book, and thus belongs to that genre of academic literature that sells best and is nowadays mainly encountered in the form of textbooks and handbooks. The intentionally uncomplicated language—the book was addressed to a wide audience, and Berger "avoided as much as possible the technical dialect for which sociologists have earned a dubious notoriety" (ibid., vii)—and the humor with which he presents sociology as a kind of "royal game" (loc. cit.), also played a part in ensuring that the book reached such a large number of readers outside the field of sociology. *Invitation to Sociology* is the work in which Berger most clearly expresses what he himself describes as his humanistic standpoint, namely his belief that sociology by its nature belongs to the humanities—a belief that was influenced by the phenomenology of Alfred Schutz.

The Sacred Canopy (1967) was also a commercial and academic success. As with *The Social Construction of Reality* (1966a) and *Invitation to Sociology* (1963a), it was in tune with the then prevailing sociological description of social change. This was due, especially, to the secularization thesis elaborated in the second part of the book. However, Berger (2011: 100) notes that, in contrast to the other two "minor classics," "if I were to rewrite it, I would not leave the text as it is." He criticizes the fact that the language was "unnecessarily complicated" (which he considers to be a common vice among sociologists) and that the second part—on secularization—was simply wrong. The book was read more as a monumental example of his substantial conception of religion—as opposed to the functionalist perspective adopted by Luckmann in *Invisible Religion* (1967)—than as a concretization of his theory for the sociology of knowledge on the basis of religion.

The basic theme of Berger's sociology—the tension between the objective and the subjective aspects of human experience of the social order, between structure and action, and between coercion and freedom—was already perceptible in *The Precarious Vision* (1961b). This book distinguishes between *faith* and *religion*; it attempts to debunk social fictions with the help of Christian faith, and to unmask the religious legitimation of these social fictions (2011: 73). Berger argues that—in contrast to the typical legitimating function of religion—a Christian faith committed to truth precisely does not contribute to validating and sanctifying social roles. In this sense, faith has more or less the same effect as anti-religious criticism:

> Christian faith puts in question the assumptions, the self-righteousness, and with these the bad faith of the social carnival. The pretensions of the masquerade collapse in the encounter with the God of truth. (1961b: 172–73)

Berger pulls no punches in *The Precarious Vision* (1961b), especially when it comes to choosing illustrative examples. With resounding clarity, he points out in this early work that religion serves as a means of social control and as a moral alibi—for capital punishment, for example. He uses Jean-Paul Sartre's term "bad faith" (*mauvaise foi*) to describe the attitude, supported in particular by bureaucratic structures, that one has no choice, that one is not responsible for one's actions, that one is merely doing one's duty. And he argues that:

> Bad faith is so important because it is the other side of freedom. Bad faith is the denial of freedom, because it deludes men into thinking that they have no choice in a situation. In reality, there are very few situations indeed where the words "no option" are literally true. At the very least, as the Stoics knew, there is the choice of death. (ibid., 94)

In sociological usage, precarious means not only lacking in stability but also doubtful. This doubtfulness shatters the apparent certainty of political and religious convictions. Hence, in its ethical dimension, too, precariousness is just another word for what Berger and Zijderveld praise as doubt in a book they coauthored in 2009.

In Praise of Doubt (Berger & Zijderveld 2009) is subtitled *How to Have Convictions without Becoming a Fanatic*. In this book, the authors offer ethical instructions on how to find a middle position between relativism and fundamentalism. Their six-point program (2009: 116ff.) can be summarized as follows: 1. Differentiate between the core of the position and more marginal components. 2. Recognize the historical context of your tradition. 3. Reject relativism to balance out the rejection of fundamentalism. 4. Accept doubt as having a positive role in a community of belief. 5. Do not categorize as enemies those who do not share your worldview. 6. Develop and maintain institutions of civil society that enable peaceful debate and conflict solution.

According to Berger and Zijderveld, in an age where there are fewer and fewer absolute certainties within the taken-for-granted worldview, doubt with respect to political and religious convictions engenders a moderate—inclusivist—attitude. This attitude is characterized by the fact that it "affirm[s] strongly the truth-claims of one tradition [while] accepting possibilities of truth in other traditions" (ibid., 49). The authors argue that, under conditions of modernity, absolute certainty prevails only in the area of fundamental moral convictions. This certainty finds expression, for example, in the Golden Rule ("that one should not do to another what is despicable to oneself" (ibid., 124)), and in Article 1 of the constitution of the Federal Republic of Germany—"The dignity of man is inviolate." Hence their assertion that "there are cognitive and moral limits to doubt" (ibid., 121).

For Berger and Zijderveld, doubt is not merely the opposite of certainty. Rather, as Berger put it in a radio interview with Daniele Rehm in 2009, he and his coauthor conceive of doubt as the "willingness to take positions even if you're not completely certain." Berger and Zijderveld (ibid., 46) point out that "What concerns us in this book is that group who are in quest of an authority that will declare an absolutely, ultimately correct choice."

Although reality and knowledge are the key terms, and the basic theme of *The Social Construction of Reality* (1966a: 1), the concept of certainty also plays an important role. This is due to the fact that it is central to Berger and Luckmann's definition of reality, which they conceive of as the "certainty that phenomena are real and that they possess specific characteristics" (loc. cit.). In contrast to the central focus of the new sociology of knowledge, namely, reality and knowledge, Berger and Zijderveld (2009) take up a basic theme of the *classical* sociology of knowledge—truth and relativism—and thereby enter epistemological territory.

With an attitude of fundamental skepticism vis-à-vis all -isms, regardless of their provenance, Berger and Zijderveld prevent the pendulum from swinging from one extreme (fundamentalism) to the other (relativism). They argue that, in postmodernist discourse in particular, the relativization of certainties threatens to turn into an ethic of "anything goes" that eschews moral judgments and the acknowledgement of the moral necessity of values. The authors' distaste for postmodernist theories that replace truth with narrations is motivated not least by the fact that these theories question facts that are obvious common sense. They argue:

> In short, one can doubt big and important, or small and unimportant, things. One can harbor doubts about oneself, the world at large, or God. What these cases have in common is that they question whether something or someone is reliable, trustworthy, and meaningful—that is, whether something or someone is "true." Doubt and truth, in other words, are about relationships. (ibid., 105)

If relativity is to be considered the central problem of the sociology of knowledge, and "morality and religion have been the two areas in which the effects of modern relativity have been most shattering, for reasons that are not hard to grasp" (Berger & Kellner 1981: 77), then Peter L. Berger has, in fact, always found himself on the rocky terrain that straddles the border between the sociology of knowledge and epistemology.

Apart from *The Social Construction of Reality* (Berger & Luckmann 1966a), which is unquestionably Berger's most important contribution to the sociology of knowledge, *The Sacred Canopy* (1967) and *The Homeless Mind* (Berger et al. 1973a) contributed to the sociology-of-knowledge foundation that shaped his later works. These books are primarily addressed to the sociological community, whereas *Invitation to Sociology* (1963a: vii) is "addressed to those who, for one reason or another, have come to wonder or to ask questions about sociology." By contrast, the target audience of *A Rumor of Angels* (1969a) comprises theologians and "religiously musical" laypeople. The special way in which Berger approaches his subject matter—and his audience—is the key to explaining the public impact that the book has achieved.

A Rumor of Angels (1969a) is groundbreaking in the sense that Berger's characteristic way of confronting the subject of religion manifests itself clearly for the first time. In this—and in all subsequent works relating to religion—he approaches his subject matter both from a sociological perspective and from the perspective of a theologically well-versed religious person. The choice of the latter perspective is informed by Berger's substantial definition of religion, which reflects "a specifically supernaturalist worldview" (2011: 97). Discussing the book in *Adventures of an Accidental Sociologist* (ibid., 101), Berger recalls:

> I made it clear that I was not speaking here as a sociologist but as a layperson without formal theological credentials. . . . The theological task . . . is to show how even in this secularized world the

supernatural may be "rediscovered." This task cannot be undertaken with the tools of sociology (or, for that matter, any other empirical science). But sociology is relevant because it can help to "relativize the relativizers"—the secular worldview, just like any religion, has a specific "plausibility structure," which, when analyzed, loses its pretension of conveying absolute truth.

Despite the fact that he keeps the two perspectives separate, this dual approach caused sociologists to view Berger with suspicion. That his target audience did not share this skepticism is evidenced by the fact that *A Rumor of Angels* was a resounding success. In his career memoir (2011: 101–2) he notes, "It was my last truly successful book of the sixties (and, to date, of any subsequent period). It too is till in print, with nine foreign translations, including (surprisingly for a book of Christian theology) into Japanese and Bahasa Indonesia." Berger explains that he never could understand why translations of most of his major books were published by a Muslim publishing house in Indonesia, until he met the publishers on a visit to Jakarta: "As believing Muslims they were intrigued by an author who looked at religion from an empirical perspective and nevertheless affirmed his own religious faith (never mind that it was Christian)" (loc. cit.).

A closer analysis of Berger's approach to the treatment of religion and the "quest for faith" (the title of a book he published in 2004) reveals that he assumes three roles, and, as a rule, separates them clearly. He speaks as a sociologist, as a theologically informed layperson, and as a confessed Christian. As a sociologist of religion, he concerns himself with the constructed nature of religious systems. In other words, he takes a sociology-of-knowledge approach to this subject matter. However, the sociology of knowledge—and sociology in general—cannot assess the validity of a religious experience or an account of such an experience. On the contrary, it can concern itself only with empirically graspable phenomena. Berger does not conclude from this that the subject matter of the sociology of religion can, or should, be limited to the social context, origins, functions, and manifestations of religion. Rather, a sociologist of religion can attempt to furnish a phenomenological description of religious experience. Nonetheless, as Berger and Kellner (1981: 87) stress, when so doing, the ontological character of the religious experiences described in the verbal and written accounts to which one has access must be rigorously bracketed. In other words, what is of relevance to the sociology of religion is the *noetic* aspect of religious experience—that is, the way in which

134

the act of consciousness (believing) refers to its object. The *noematic* aspect of religious experience—that is, the way in which the object (the believed) appears through the noetic act—is shown only within brackets in the phenomenological description (cf. Berger & Kellner 1981: 87). By removing the brackets and confirming the ontological status of what is believed, one switches to a religious frame of reference and takes on the role of believer.

As a confessed Christian, Berger struggles with the possibility of faith in an "age of credulity" (cf. the subtitle of *A Far Glory* (1992b)). In *A Far Glory*, he argues, following Blaise Pascal, that insofar as the existence of God is by definition "that which one does not know," faith is a wager that God exists. Berger's message, which is related to Kierkegaard's "leap of faith" (cf. Berger 1979: 74), is that, while we cannot obtain certainty in this matter, those who believe gain something more—the belief in the validity of joy.

As a theologically informed layperson who was dissatisfied with the reactions of theologians to the signs of the times, Berger sought "contemporary possibilities of religious affirmation"—the subtitle of *The Heretical Imperative* (1979). As mentioned in Chapter 3 above, his preferred option, "the inductive possibility," has an anthropological starting point and proceeds inductively from everyday human experiences, which he calls "signals of transcendence" (1969a: 53). This option renders inductive, empirically based faith conceivable.

Prisching (2001: 34) regards Berger as a "second-order relationist" for whom, in contrast to Karl Mannheim, several existential determinations—and roles—can exist side by side. He doubts whether *truth* can be recognized if one switches between determinations. Berger would disagree. He claims "dual citizenship"—as a sociologist, on the one hand, and as a theological and political actor and religious believer on the other. And he contends (in Brix & Prisching 2001: 167; our translation) that "role contamination" is by no means inevitable, insofar as several perspectives can exist side by side: "The coherence of one perspective does not rule out the coherence of the other."

This coherence is facilitated by the fact that, in the preface to his books and lectures, Berger always outlines his frames of reference. He clarifies the role(s)—sociologist, theologically and politically informed layperson, and/or moralist—that he intends to assume. He proves himself a highly reflective and self-deprecating role player. And he is serious when he maintains that the positions that he assumes when he thinks, says, or writes something are standpoints that one can adopt, and that one can abandon. With the exception of his own fundamental moral values, which are non-negotiable, he regards these positions as tentative. Hence, although he presents his propositions in a compelling and persuasive way, he is never dogmatic. In my view, this explains the impact that Peter L. Berger's books have achieved.

Note

1. "Perhaps the word 'construction' in the Berger/Luckmann volume was unfortunate, as it suggests a creation ex nihilo—as if one said, 'There is nothing here but our constructions.' But this was not the authors' intention. They were far too much influenced by Durkheim to subscribe to such a view. What they proposed was that all reality was subject to socially derived interpretations. What much of postmodernist theory proposes is that all interpretations are equally valid—which, of course, would spell the end of any scientific approach to human history and society. And some postmodern theorists have maintained that nothing exists except or outside these interpretations—which comes close to the clinical definition of schizophrenia, a condition in which one is unable to distinguish reality from one's fantasies" (Berger & Zijderveld 2009: 66).

References

I Publications by Peter L. Berger

1954a   *The Bahá'i Movement. A Sociological Interpretation*, New York, unpublished PhD dissertation, New School for Social Research.

1954b   The Sociological Study of Sectarianism, *Social Research*, 21, 4: 467–485.

1955   Demythologization: Crisis in Continental Theology, *Review of Religion*, 59, 20: 5–24.

1958   Sectarianism and Religious Sociation, *American Journal of Sociology*, 64, 1: 41–44.

1960   (& Richard Lieban) Kulturelle Wertstruktur und Bestattungspraktiken in den Vereinigten Staaten, *Kölner Zeitschrift für Soziologie und Sozialpsychologie*, 12: 224–263.

1961a   *The Noise of Solemn Assemblies: Christian Commitment and the Religious Establishment in America*, Garden City NY: Doubleday. [German: *Kirche ohne Auftrag: am Beispiel Amerikas.* Stuttgart: Kreuz 1962].

1961b   *The Precarious Vision: A Sociologist Looks at Social Fictions and Christian Faith*, Garden City, NY: Doubleday.

1962a   (& Dennison Nash) The Child, the Family and the ›Religious Revival‹ in Suburbia, *Journal for the Scientific Study of Religion*, 1: 85–93.

1962b   Church Commitment in an American Suburb: An Analysis of the Decision to Join, *Archives of the Sociology of Religion*, 13: 105–120.

1963a   *Invitation to Sociology. A Humanistic Perspective.* Garden City, NY, Doubleday. [German: *Einladung zur Soziologie. Eine humanistische Perspektive,* Olten: Walter 1969].

1963b   Charisma and Religious Innovation. The Social Location of Israelite Prophecy, *American Sociological Review*, 28, 6: 940–950.

1963c   A Market Model for the Analysis of Ecumenicity, *Social Research*, 30: 77–93 [German: Ein Marktmodell zur Analyse ökumenischer Prozesse, *Internationales Jahrbuch für Religionssoziologie I*, 1965, 235–249].

1963d   (& Thomas Luckmann) Sociology of Religion and Sociology of Knowledge, *Sociology and Social Research*, 47: 417–427.

1964a   (Ed.) *The Human Shape of Work: Studies in the Sociology of Occupations*, New York: Macmillan.

1964b   (& Thomas Luckmann) Social Mobility and Personal Identity, *European Journal of Sociology*, 2, 5: 331–343.

1965a   *The Enclaves*, Garden City, NY: Doubleday [novel written under the pseudonym Felix Bastian].

1965b   Towards a Sociological Understanding of Psychoanalysis, *Social Research*, 32: 26–41.

1965c   (& Hansfried Kellner) Arnold Gehlen and the Theory of Institutions, *Social Research*, 32, 1: 110–115.

1965d   (& Hansfried Kellner) Die Ehe und die Konstruktion der Wirklichkeit. Eine Abhandlung zur Mikrosoziologie des Wissens, *Soziale Welt*, 16: 220–235.

1965e   (& Stanley Pullberg) Reification and the Sociological Critique of Consciousness, *History and Theory*, 4: 196–211 [German: Verdinglichung und die soziologische Kritik des Bewusstseins, in: H. Lieber (ed.), *Ideologie – Wissenschaft – Gesellschaft. Neuere Beiträge zur Diskussion*, Darmstadt 1976].

1966a   (& Thomas Luckmann), *The Social Construction of Reality: A Treatise in the Sociology of Knowledge*, Garden City, NY: Doubleday. [German: *Die gesellschaftliche Konstruktion der Wirklichkeit*, Frankfurt: Fischer 1969].

1966b   Identity as a Problem in the Sociology of Knowledge, *European Journal of Sociology*, 7, 1: 105–115.

1966c   (& Thomas Luckmann) Secularization and Pluralism, *International Yearbook for the Sociology of Religion 2*, 73–86.

1967   *The Sacred Canopy: Elements of a Sociological Theory of Religion*, Garden City, NY: Doubleday; from 1969: *The Social Reality of Religion*. [German.: *Zur Dialektik von Religion und Gesellschaft. Elemente einer soziologischen Theorie*, Frankfurt: Fischer 1973].

1969a   *A Rumor of Angels: Modern Society and the Rediscovery of the Supernatural*, Garden City NY: Doubleday. [German: *Auf den Spuren der Engel. Die moderne Gesellschaft und die Wiederentdeckung der Transzendenz*, Frankfurt: Fischer 1970].

1969b   (Ed.) *Marxism and Sociology: Views from Eastern Europe*, New York: Appleton Century Crofts.

1970a   (& Richard J. Neuhaus) (eds) *Movement and Revolution. On American Radicalism*, Garden City, N.Y.: Doubleday. [German: *Protestbewegung und Revolution oder die Verantwortung der Radikalen*, Frankfurt: Fischer 1971].

1970b   The Problem of Multiple Realities: Alfred Schutz and Robert Musil, in M. Natanson, *Phenomenology and Social Reality. Essays in Memory of Alfred Schutz*, The Hague: Nijhoff: 213–233.

1971a   Soziologische Betrachtungen über die Zukunft der Religion. Zum gegenwärtigen Stand der Säkularisierungsdebatte, in O. Schatz, *Hat die Religion Zukunft?*, Graz: Styria: 49–68.

1971b   Secularization and the Problem of Plausibility, in: K. Thompson, J. Tunstall, *Sociological Perspectives*, Harmondsworth: Penguin Books: 446–459.

1972   (& Brigitte Berger) *Sociology – A Biographical Approach*, New York: Basic Books. [German: *Individuum & Co. – Soziologie beginnt beim Nachbarn*, Stuttgart: Deutsche Verlags-Anstalt 1974; *Wir und die Gesellschaft. Eine Einführung in die Soziologie – entwickelt an der Alltagserfahrung*, Reinbek bei Hamburg: Rowohlt 1976].

1973a   (& Brigitte Berger & Hansfried Kellner) *The Homeless Mind. Modernization and Consciousness*. New York: Random House. [German.: *Das Unbehagen in der Modernität*, Frankfurt, New York: Campus 1975].

| 1973b | (& Brigitte Berger and Hansfried Kellner) Demodernizing Consciousness, *Social Policy*, 3, 6: 3–19. |

1973b   (& Brigitte Berger and Hansfried Kellner) Demodernizing Consciousness, *Social Policy*, 3, 6: 3–19.

1974a   *Pyramids of Sacrifice: Political Ethics and Social Change*, New York: Basic Books. [German: *Welt der Reichen, Welt der Armen: Politische Ethik und sozialer Wandel*, Munich: List 1976].

1974b   *Religion in a Revolutionary Society*, Washington, DC: American Enterprise Institute for Public Policy Research.

1974c   Some Second Thoughts on Substantive Versus Functional Definitions of Religion, *Journal for the Scientific Study of Religion*, 13, 2: 125–133.

1975   *Protocol of a Damnation: A Novel*, New York: Seabury Press.

1976a   (& Richard J. Neuhaus) (eds) *Against the World for the World: The Hartford Appeal and the Future of American Religion*, New York: Seabury.

1976b   In Praise of Particularity: The Concept of Mediating Structures, *Review of Politics*, 38, 3: 399–410.

1976c   (& Richard J. Neuhaus) The Hartford Appeal for Theological Affirmation, in: Berger & Neuhaus (eds), 1–7.

1976d   For a world with windows. Hartford in sociocultural context, in: Berger & Neuhaus (eds), 8–19.

1977a   *Facing up to Modernity: Excursions in Society, Politics and Religion*, New York: Basic Books.

1977b   A Signal of Transcendence, in: 1977a: 258–268.

1979   *The Heretical Imperative: Contemporary Possibilities of Religious Affirmation*, Garden City, NY: Anchor Press. [German: *Religion: Der Zwang zur Häresie. Religion in der pluralistischen Gesellschaft*, Frankfurt: Fischer 1980].

1980   (Ed.) *The Other Side of God: A Polarity in World Religions*, Garden City, NY: Doubleday.

1981   (& Hansfried Kellner) *Sociology Reinterpreted. An Essay on Method and Vocation*, Garden City NY: Anchor Press/Doubleday. [German.: *Für eine neue Soziologie. Ein Essay über Methode und Profession*, Frankfurt: Fischer 1984].

1983a   (& Brigitte Berger) *The War over the Family: Capturing the Middle Ground*, Garden City, NY: Anchor Press/ Doubleday. [German: *In Verteidigung der bürgerlichen Familie*, Frankfurt: Fischer 1984].

1983b   Das Problem der mannigfaltigen Wirklichkeiten. Alfred Schütz und Robert Musil, in: R. Grathoff, B. Waldenfels (eds), *Sozialität und Intersubjektivität*, Munich: Fink, 229–251.

1986a   *The Capitalist Revolution: Fifty Propositions about Prosperity, Equality, and Liberty*, New York: Basic Books. [German: *Die kapitalistische Revolution: Fünfzig Leitsätze über Wohlstand, Gleichheit und Freiheit*, Vienna: Ed. Atelier 1992].

1986b   (& Philipp Moreno) (eds) *The Arithmetic of Justice: Capitalism and Equality in America*, Lanham: University Press of America.

1986c   A Sociological View of the Antismoking Phenomenon, in: R. Tollison, *Smoking and Society: Toward a Balanced Assessment*, Lexington, MA: Lexington Books: 225–240.

1986d   Epilogue, in: J. Hunter, S. Ainlay, *Making Sense in Modern Times: Peter L. Berger and the Vision of Interpretive Sociology*, London and New York: Routledge and Kegan Paul: 221–235.

1987a   (Ed.) *Modern Capitalism Vol I: Capitalism and Equality in America*, Boston: Hamilton.

1987b   (Ed.) *Modern Capitalism Vol II: Capitalism and Equality in the Third World*, Boston: Hamilton.

1988a   (& Bobby Godsell) (eds) *A Future South Africa: Visions, Strategies and Realities*, Boulder: Westview.

1988b   (& Hsing-Huang Michael Hsiao) (eds) *In Search of an East Asian Development Model*, New Brunswick, NJ: Transaction Publishers.

1988c   Robert Musil und die Errettung des Ich, *Zeitschrift für Soziologie*, 17, 2: 132–142 [also in P. Berger, *Sehnsucht nach Sinn*, 1994, 111–127].

1988d   Environmental Tobacco Smoke: Ideological Issue and Cultural Issue, in R. Tollison, *Clearing the Air: Perspectives on Environmental Tobacco Smoke*, Lexington, D.C. Heath and Company: 85–86.

1990   (Ed.) *The Capitalist Spirit: Toward a Religious Ethic of Wealth Creation*, San Francisco: ICS Press.

1991   (& Digby Anderson, Robert Browning, Peter Finch, Raymond Johnstone, Irving Kristol, James Le Fanu, Mark Mills, Petr Skrabanek, Aaron Wildavsky) (eds) *Health, Lifestyle and the Environment: Countering the Panic. Symposium: Selected Papers*, London: Social Affairs Unit.

1992a   *Democracy and Capitalism* (booklet), Johannesburg: Urban Foundation.

1992b   *A Far Glory: The Quest of Faith in an Age of Credulity*, New York: Free Press. [German: *Sehnsucht nach Sinn: Glauben in einer Zeit der Leichtgläubigkeit*, Frankfurt: Campus 1994].

1993   (Ed.) *Institutions of Democracy and Development (A Sequoia Seminar)*, San Francisco: ICS Press.

1994   Does Sociology Still Make Sense? *Schweizerische Zeitschrift für Soziologie*, 20, 1: 3–12 [Abbreviated version of: Sociology: A Disinvitation?, *Society*, 30, 1992: 12–18].

1995a   (& Thomas Luckmann), *Modernity, Pluralism and the Crisis of Meaning*, Gütersloh: Bertelsmann Foundation Publishers. [German: *Modernität, Pluralismus und Sinnkrise. Die Orientierung des modernen Menschen*, Gütersloh: Verlag Bertelsmann Stiftung 1995].

1995b   *Weltethos und Protestantismus*, Hannover: Ev. Luth. Kirchenamt.

1996   (& Richard J. Neuhaus) *To Empower People: From State to Civil Society*, Washington, DC: American Enterprise Institute Press.

1997a   *Redeeming Laughter: The Comic Dimension of Human Experience*, Berlin: de Gruyter. [German.: *Erlösendes Lachen. Das Komische in der menschlichen Erfahrung*, Berlin: de Gruyter 1998].

1997b   (Ed.) *The Limits of Social Cohesion. Conflict and Mediation in Pluralist Societies. A Report of the Bertelsmann Foundation to the Club of Rome*, Boulder, CO: Westview. [German: *Die Grenzen der Gemeinschaft: Konflikt und Vermittlung in pluralistischen Gesellschaften. Ein Bericht der Bertelsmann Stiftung an den Club of Rome*, Gütersloh: Verlag Bertelsmann Stiftung 1997].

1997c   Epistemological modesty: An interview with Peter Berger, *Christian Century*, 114: 972– 978.

1997d   Four Faces of Global Culture, *The National Interest*, 49: 23–29. [German: Die vier Gesichter der globalen Kultur, *Europäische Rundschau*, 26, 1: 105–113, 1998].

1998a   (& Ann Bernstein) (eds) *Business and Democracy. Cohabitation or Contradiction?*, London: Pinter.

1998b   Sola fide. Betrachtungen eines Soziologen, in *Auf den Spuren der Theologie. Ansprachen anlässlich der Verleihung der Ehrendoktorwürde an Peter L. Berger*, Zurich: Pano, 21–37.

1999   (ed.) *The Desecularization of the World: Resurgent Religion and World Politics*, Washington, DC: Ethics and Public Policy Center.

2001a   Mit merkwürdigen Gefühlen – ein Nachwort, in: M. Prisching (ed.), *Gesellschaft verstehen*, Vienna: Passagen, 165–173.

2001b   Reflections on Sociology of Religion Today, *Sociology of Religion*, 62, 4: 425–429.

2002a   (& Samuel P. Huntington) (eds) *Many Globalizations: Cultural Diversity in the Contemporary World*, Oxford: Oxford University Press.

2002b   Secularization and De-Secularization, in L. Woodhead et al., *Religions in the Modern World. Traditions and Transformations*, London, New York: Routledge, 291–298.

2004a   *Questions of Faith: A Skeptical Affirmation of Christianity (Religion and the Modern World)*, Malden, Mass: Blackwell. [German: *Erlösender Glaube? Fragen an das Christentum*, Berlin: de Gruyter 2006].

2004b   Max Weber is Alive and Well, and Living in Guatemala: The Protestant Ethic Today, New York: Cornell University Paper presented to the 100th Anniversary Conference, Centre for the Study of Economy and Society.

2005   Religion and the West, *National Interest*, 75, 80: 112–119.

2008a   *Im Morgenlicht der Erinnerung. Eine Kindheit in turbulenter Zeit*, Vienna: Molden.

2008b   (& Grace Davie & Effie Fokas) *Religious America, Secular Europe? A Theme and Variations*, Aldershot: Ashgate.

2008c   (& Wallace L. Daniel & Christopher Marsh) (eds) *Perspectives on Church-State Relations in Russia*, Waco, TX: Baylor University.

2008d   *Faith and Development: A global perspective*, Johannesburg: The Centre for Development and Enterprise.

2009   (& Anton Zijderveld) *In Praise of Doubt. How to Have Conviction without Becoming a Fanatic*, New York: Harper One [German: *Lob des Zweifels. Was ein überzeugender Glaube braucht*, Freiburg: Herder 2010].

2011   *Adventures of an Accidental Sociologist. How to Explain the World without Becoming a Bore*. Amherst, New York: Prometheus Books.

II Publications about Peter L. Berger, other References

Berger, Brigitte (1971), *Societies in Change: An Introduction to Comparative Sociology*, New York London: Basic Books.

Beck, Ulrich (1983), Jenseits von Stand und Klasse? Soziale Ungleichheiten, gesellschaftliche Individualisierungsprozesse und die Entstehung neuer sozialer Formationen und Identitäten, in Reinhard Kreckel (ed.), *Soziale Ungleichheiten*, Sonderband 2 der Sozialen Welt, Göttingen: Schwatz, 35–74.

Brix, Emil & Prisching, Manfred (2001), Persönliches und Gesellschaftliches. Ein Gespräch mit Peter L. Berger, in M. Prisching (ed.), *Gesellschaft verstehen*, Vienna: Passagen, 165–173.

Dobbelaere, Karel & Lauwers, Jan (1973), Definition of Religion. A Sociological Critique, *Social Compass*, 20, 4: 535–551.

Dreher, Jochen (2007), Lebenswelt, Identität und Gesellschaft – Sozialtheoretische Reflexionen zwischen Phänomenologie, Wissenssoziologie und empirischer Forschung, in T. Luckmann, *Lebenswelt, Identität und Gesellschaft*, Konstanz: UVK, 7–23.

Durkheim, Emile (1938 [1895]), *The Rules of Sociological Method*, Chicago: University of Chicago Press (trans. Solovay, Sarah A., Mueller, John M., ed. Catlin, George E.G.).

———. (1965 [1892]), *Montesquieu and Rousseau: Forerunners of Sociology*. Ann Arbor: University of Michigan Press.

Eisermann, Gottfried (1960), Einleitung, in: W. Stark, *Die Wissenssoziologie*, Stuttgart: Enke, V–XI.

Eliade, Mircea (1957), *Das Heilige und das Profane*, Hamburg: Rowohlt.

Endress, Martin (2007), Max Weber, in: R. Schützeichel (ed.), *Handbuch Wissenssoziologie und Wissensforschung*, Konstanz: UVK, 42–54.

Fuller, Robert C. (1987), Religion and Empiricism in the Works of Peter Berger, *Zygon*, 22, 4: 497–510.

Gaede, Stan D. (1981), Review Symposium of ›The Heretical Imperative‹, *Journal for the Scientific Study of Religion*, 20, 2, 181–185.

———. (1986), Excursus: The Problem of Truth, in J. Hunter, S. Ainlay (eds), *Making Sense in Modern Times: Peter L. Berger and the Vision of Interpretive Sociology*, London, New York: Routledge and Kegan Paul, 159–175.

Goffman, Erving (1971), *Relations in Microstudies of the Public Order*, New York: Basic Books.

Grossman, Nathan J. D. (1975), On Peter Berger's Definition of Religion, *Journal for the Scientific Study of Religion*, 14, 3: 289–292.

Gurwitsch, Aron (1971), Einführung, in A. Schütz, *Gesammelte Aufsätze. Vol. 1*, Den Haag: Nijhoff, XV–XXXVIII.

Hammond, Phillip E. (1986), Religion in the modern world, in J. Hunter, S. Ainlay, C. Stephen (eds), *Making Sense of Modern Times. Peter L. Berger and the Vision of Interpretive Sociology*, London, New York: Routledge, 143–158.

Hefner, Robert (2000), *Civil Islam: Muslims and Democratization in Indonesia*, Princeton, NJ: Princeton University Press.

Hitzler, Ronald (1988), *Sinnwelten. Ein Beitrag zum Verstehen von Kultur*, Opladen: Westdeutscher

———. (1999), Konsequenzen der Situationsdefinition, in R. Hitzler, J. Reichertz & N. Schröer (eds), *Hermeneutische Wissenssoziologie*, Konstanz: UVK, 289–308.

Honer, Anne (1999), Bausteine zu einer lebensweltorientierten Wissenssoziologie, in R. Hitzler, J. Reichertz & N. Schröer (eds), *Hermeneutische Wissenssoziologie*, Konstanz: UVK, 51–67.

Hunter, James D. & Ainlay, Stephen C. (eds) (1986), *Making Sense of Modern Times. Peter L. Berger and the Vision of Interpretive Sociology*, London, New York: Routledge.

James, William (2007 [1890]), The Perception of Reality, *The Principles of Psychology*, 2, New York: Cosimo.

Kaesler, Dirk (1999), Was sind und zu welchem Ende studiert man die Klassiker der Soziologie?, in Dirk Kaesler (ed.), *Klassiker der Soziologie* Vol. 1, Munich: Beck, 11–38.

Kaufmann, Jean-Claude (1994), *Schmutzige Wäsche. Zur ehelichen Konstruktion von Alltag*, Konstanz: UVK.

Kieserling, André (2010), Die zwei Soziologien des Wissens, in A. Honer, M. Meuser & M. Pfadenhauer (eds), *Fragile Sozialität*, Wiesbaden: VS, 433–444.

Knoblauch, Hubert (2005), *Wissenssoziologie*, Konstanz: UTB.

———. (2007), Phänomenologisch fundierte Wissenssoziologie, in: R. Schützeichel (ed.), *Handbuch Wissenssoziologie und Wissensforschung*, Konstanz: UVK, 118–126.

König, René (1976): Emile Durkheim. Der Soziologe als Moralist, in: D. Kaesler (ed.), *Klassiker des soziologischen Denkens*, Vol. 1, Munich: Beck, 312–364.

Lieber, Hans-Joachim (1952), *Wissen und Gesellschaft*, Tübingen: Niemeyer.

Luckmann, Thomas (1967), *The Invisible Religion*, New York: MacMillan.

———. (1969), *Secolarizzazione: un mito contemporaneo*, in *Cultura e Politica*, 14, 175–182.

———. (1983): *Life-World and Social Realities*. Portsmouth: Heinemann. [German: *Lebenswelt, Identität und Gesellschaft*, Konstanz: UVK 2007].

———. (1985), Über die Funktion der Religion, in P. Koslowski (ed.), *Die religiöse Dimension der Gesellschaft. Religion und ihre Theorien*, Tübingen: Mohr, 26–41.

———. (1986), Grundformen der gesellschaftlichen Vermittlung des Wissens: Kommunikative Gattungen, in: F. Neihardt, R. Lepsius & J. Weiß (eds), *Kultur und Gesellschaft*, Sonderheft 27 der KZfSS, Opladen: Westdeutscher, 191–211.

———. (1995), Gespräch mit Prof. Dr. Thomas (Tomaž) Luckmann, in: M. M. Zalaznik (ed.), Begegnungen, Ljubljana: Založba Nova revija, 59–68 (trans. Peter Scherber).

———. (1999), Wirklichkeiten: individuelle Konstitution und gesellschaftliche Konstruktion, in: R. Hitzler, J. Reichertz & N. Schröer (eds), *Hermeneutische Wissenssoziologie*, Konstanz: UVK, 17–28.

———. (2001), Berger and his collaborator(s), in L. Woodhead, P. Heelas & D. Martin (eds), *Peter Berger and the Study of Religion*, London, New York: Routledge, 17–25.

———. (2007a), Über die Grenzen der Sozialwelt, in Thomas Luckmann, *Lebenswelt, Identität und Gesellschaft*, Konstanz: UVK, 62–90.

McCarthy, E. Doyle (1996), *Knowledge as Culture: The New Sociology of Knowledge*, London.

Mechling, Jay (1986), The Jamesian Berger, in J. Hunter, S. Ainlay (ed.), *Making Sense in Modern Times: Peter L. Berger and the Vision of Interpretive Sociology*, London, New York: Routledge and Kegan Paul, 197–220.

143

Mills, C. Wright (1959), *The Sociological Imagination*, New York: Oxford University Press.

Musil, Robert (1995 [1930ff.]), *The Man Without Qualities*, (trans. Burton Pike and Sophie Wilkins). New York: Knopf. [German: *Der Mann ohne Eigenschaften*, Vol. 1 Berlin 1930, Vol. 2 Berlin 1932, Vol. 3 Lausanne 1943].

Otto, Rudolf (1963), *Das Heilige. Über das Irrationale in der Idee des Göttlichen und sein Verhältnis zum Rationalen*, Munich: Beck (EA 1917).

Oldenbourg, Zoé (1979), *Argile et Cendres*, Paris Gallimard (EA 1946).

Pfadenhauer, Michaela (1998), Rollenkompetenz. Träger, Spieler und Professionelle als Akteure für die hermeneutische Wissenssoziologie, in R. Hitzler, J. Reichertz & N. Schröer (eds) *Hermeneutische Wissenssoziologie*, Konstanz: UVK, 267–285.

———. (2003), *Professionalität. Eine wissenssoziologische Rekonstruktion institutionalisierter Kompetenzdarstellungskompetenz*, Opladen: Leske + Budrich.

Plessner, Helmuth (1982), Die Stufen des Organischen und der Mensch, in Helmuth Plessner *Gesammelte Schriften Vol. IV*, Frankfurt: Suhrkamp.

———. (1985), Abwandlungen des Ideologiegedankens [first published 1931], in H. Plessner, *Schriften zur Soziologie und Sozialphilosophie. Gesammelte Schriften Bd. X*, Frankfurt: Suhrkamp, 41–70.

Prisching, Manfred (2001), *Gesellschaft verstehen. Peter L. Berger und die Soziologie der Gegenwart*, Vienna: Passagen.

Reichertz, Jo (2006), Läßt sich die Plausibilität wissenssoziologischer Empirie selbst wieder plausibilisieren? Oder: Über den Versuch, den Bus zu schieben, in: D. Tänzler, H. Knoblauch & H.-G. Soeffner (eds), *Neue Perspektiven der Wissenssoziologie*, Konstanz: UVK, 293–315.

Rotterdam, Erasmus von (1986), *Lob der Torheit*, Ditzingen: Reclam (EA 1509).

Scheler, Max (1980), *Problems of a Sociology of Knowledge*, London: Routledge & Kegan Paul.

Schelting, Alexander von Schelting (1934), *Max Webers Wissenschaftslehre*, Tübingen: Mohr.

Schnettler, Bernt (2006), *Thomas Luckmann*, Klassiker der Wissenssoziologie, Volume 1, Konstanz: UVK.

Schutz, Alfred (1976), Some Equivocations in the Notion of Responsibility, in: A. Brodersen (ed.), 274–276. [German: Einige Äquivokationen im Begriff der Verantwortlichkeit, in A. Schütz: Gesammelte Aufsätze, Vol. 2, Den Haag: Nijhoff 1972, 256–258].

Schutz, Alfred & Luckmann, Thomas (1973), The Structures of the Life-World, Volume 1, Evanston, Illinois: Northwestern University Press. [German: *Strukturen der Lebenswelt*, Frankfurt: Suhrkamp (new one-volume UTB edition) 2003].

Schutz, Alfred & Natanson, M. A. (1982), *Collected Papers: The Problem of Social Reality*, The Hague; Boston: Nijhoff.

Shibutani, Tamotsu (1955): Reference Groups as Perspectives, *American Journal of Sociology* 60, 562–568.

Soeffner, Hans-Georg (1989), Prämissen der sozialwissenschaftlichen Hermeneutik, in H.-G. Soeffner, *Auslegung des Alltags – Alltag der Auslegung*, Frankfurt: Suhrkamp, 66–97.

———. (2000), *Gesellschaft ohne Baldachin*, Weilerswist: Velbrück Wissenschaft.

Srubar, Ilja (1979), Die Theorie der Typenbildung bei Alfred Schütz. Ihre Bedeutung und ihre Grenzen, in: W. Sprondel & R. Grathoff (eds), *Alfred Schütz und die Idee des Alltags in den Sozialwissenschaften*, Stuttgart: Enke, 43–64.

Stagl, Justin (2001), Das Unbehagen in der modernen Welt, in M. Prisching (ed.), *Gesellschaft verstehen*, Vienna: Passagen, 71–82.

Stark, Werner (1991 [1958]), *The Sociology of Knowledge: An Essay in Aid of a Deeper Understanding of the History of Ideas*, New Brunswick, New Jersey: Transaction Publishers.

Tänzler, Dirk (2006), Von der Seinsgebundenheit zum Seinsverhältnis. Wissenssoziologie zwischen Gesellschaftstheorie und Hermeneutik der Kulturen, in D. Tänzler, H. Knoblauch & H.-G. Soeffner (eds), *Neue Perspektiven der Wissenssoziologie*, Konstanz: UVK, 317–335.

Tänzler, Dirk, Knoblauch, Hubert & Soeffner, Hans-Georg (2006), Neue Perspektiven der Wissenssoziologie. Eine Einleitung, in Dirk Tänzler, Hubert Knoblauch & Hans-Georg Soeffner (eds), *Neue Perspektiven der Wissenssoziologie*, Konstanz: UVK, 7–14.

Wagner, Hellmut R. (1983), *Alfred Schutz. An Intellectual Biography*, Chicago, London: University of Chicago Press.

Weber, Max (1978 [1922]), *Economy and Society*, Roth, Guenther & Wittich, Claus (eds), Berkeley; Los Angeles: University of California Press.

———. (2003 [1904/05]) *The Protestant Ethic and the Spirit of Capitalism*, New York: Dover (translated by Talcott Parsons).

Weller, Robert (ed. 2005), *Civil Life, Globalization and Political Change in Asia*, London: Routledge.

Woodhead, Linda, Heelas, Paul & Martin, David (2001), *Peter Berger and the Study of Religion*, London, New York: Routledge.

Wuthnow, Robert (1986), Religion as sacred canopy, in J. Hunter and S. Ainlay (eds), *Making Sense of Modern Times. Peter L. Berger and the Vision of Interpretive Sociology*, London, New York: Routledge, 121–142.

Wuthnow, Robert, Hunter, James, Bergensen, A. & Kurzweil, Edith (1984), *Cultural Analysis. The Work of Peter L. Berger, Mary Douglas, Michel Foucault and Jürgen Habermas*, London: Routledge & Kegan Paul.

Zijderveld, Anton (1970), *The Abstract Society. A Cultural Analysis of our Time*, New York: Doubleday.

Bibliography of
Peter L. Berger's
Contributions to this Book

Reflections on the Twenty-Fifth Anniversary of *The Social Construction of Reality*.

Appeared in: Perspectives, the Theory Section newsletter of the American Sociological Association. Volume 15, Number 2, April 1992.

Pluralism, Protestantization, and the Voluntary Principle.

Appeared in: Democracy and the New Religious Pluralism. Edited by Thomas Banchoff. Oxford University Press 2007, pp. 19–29.

The Desecularization of the World: A Global Overview.

Appeared in: The Desecularization of the World. Resurgent Religion and World Politics. Edited by Peter L. Berger. Copyright © 1999 by the Ethics and Public Policy Center. Published jointly by the Ethics and Public Policy Center and Wm. B. Eerdmans Publishing Co.

Our Economic Culture.

Appeared in: The Cultural Context of Economics and Politics. Edited by T. William Boxx and Gary M. Quinlivan, pp. 71–77. Copyright © 1994 by the Center for Economic and Policy Education. University Press of America.

Identity as a Problem in the Sociology of Knowledge.

Appeared in: European Journal of Sociology, Volume 7, Issue 01 (1966), pp. 105–115. Copyright © Archives Européennes de Sociologie. Reprinted with the permission of Cambridge University Press.

Index